RECYCLE *and* **PLAY**

WHAT

THEY AT ARE

CAN AND

RECYCLE

and PLAY

Awesome DIY Zero-Waste
Projects to Make for Kids

Agnes Hsu

Inspiring | Educating | Creating | Entertaining

Brimming with creative inspiration, how-to projects, and useful information to enrich your everyday life, Quarto Knows is a favorite destination for those pursuing their interests and passions. Visit our site and dig deeper with our books into your area of interest: Quarto Creates, Quarto Cooks, Quarto Homes, Quarto Lives, Quarto Drives, Quarto Explores, Quarto Gifts, or Quarto Kids.

First Published in 2022 by Quarry Books, an imprint of The Quarto Group, 100 Cummings Center, Suite 265-D, Beverly, MA 01915, USA.
T (978) 282-9590 F (978) 283-2742 QuartoKnows.com

Quarry Books titles are also available at discount for retail, wholesale, promotional, and bulk purchase. For details, contact the Special Sales Manager by email at specialsales@quarto.com or by mail at The Quarto Group, Attn: Special Sales Manager, 100 Cummings Center, Suite 265-D, Beverly, MA 01915, USA.

10 9 8 7 6 5 4 3 2 1

ISBN: 978-0-7603-7318-7

Digital edition published in 2022
eISBN: 978-0-7603-7319-4

Library of Congress Cataloging-in-Publication Data

Names: Hsu, Agnes, author.
Title: Recycle and play : awesome DIY zero-waste projects to make for kids
  : 50 fun learning activities for ages 3-6 / Agnes Hsu.
Description: Beverly : Quarry Books, 2022. | Includes index. | Summary:
  "Recycle and Play transforms what many might consider trash-cardboard,
  bubble wrap, egg cartons, or plastic wrap-into invitations for
  zero-waste playful learning"-- Provided by publisher.
Identifiers: LCCN 2021029146 (print) | LCCN 2021029147 (ebook) | ISBN
  9780760373187 (trade paperback) | ISBN 9780760373194 (ebook)
Subjects: LCSH: Recycling (Waste, etc.) | Refuse as art material. |
  Handicraft. | Play. | Learning.
Classification: LCC TD794.5 .H75 2022 (print) | LCC TD794.5 (ebook) | DDC
  363.72/82--dc23
LC record available at https://lccn.loc.gov/2021029146
LC ebook record available at https://lccn.loc.gov/2021029147

Design: Allison Meierding
Photography: Ning Wong

Printed in China

To my husband Tim
who has supported every
single one of my wild and
crazy creative projects.

And to my adoring children,
Alia, Kian and Dashiell, who
are my biggest cheerleaders.
You inspire me to create and
share with boundless love
and devotion.

▲▲▲▲▲▲

CONTENTS

▲▲▲

INTRODUCTION

▲▲▲▲▲▲▲▲▲▲▲▲▲▲▲▲▲▲▲▲▲▲▲▲▲▲▲▲▲▲▲▲▲▲▲▲▲▲

> "Play is the highest form of research."
>
> **ALBERT EINSTEIN**

▲▲▲▲▲▲▲▲▲▲▲▲▲▲▲▲▲▲▲▲▲▲▲▲▲▲▲▲▲▲▲▲▲▲▲▲▲▲

When my daughter was in preschool, we started encouraging her to craft with recycled materials by playing with them and seeing what she could create. It later became very clear that this early focus on playing and learning led to her independent creativity in school. For example, she built an intricate town that contained an entire cardboard playground, made only from recyclable materials, for a school project.

When my middle son was three, he was obsessed with trains and slowly advanced to building intricate railway systems, tunnels, and bridges. He would spend hours organizing his trains by name, color, and size. What I didn't know at the time was that he was learning while playing! Did you know sorting is a precursor for early math? When building tracks, he was also cognitively developing. Now ten years old, he can now build the most intricate recycled cardboard mazes and can operate 3-D printers to make his own creations. I'm convinced his focus on play at a young age led to his creativity and love for building at a later age.

My third child, currently three years old, started fine motor play at a very young age by making simple recycled projects such as paper tube pompom drops. Our early focus on fine motor play led to him expertly pouring, scooping, and measuring ingredients at an advanced level. He's now able to create decadent baked goods in the kitchen.

Welcome to *Recycle and Play*

Hello and welcome to *Recycle and Play*! My name is Agnes Hsu, and first and foremost, I am a mom to three playful children, ages three, ten, and twelve. I wanted to share these personal stories about my children because I am passionate about starting play at a young age but also have the advantage of seeing its positive impact firsthand with my children. In this book, you will find fifty playful learning projects for preschool-aged children, with a focus on no-waste, recycled ideas.

I'm also the founder of a kids' creative craft website www.hellowonderful.co, founded eight years ago, and am the co-founder of the popular Recycle and Play Instagram community @RecycleandPlay. We showcase the very best recycle and play activities and, as a result, have a great understanding of the most fun and engaging recycled projects for little ones.

Why You Need This Book

Did you know that young children learn while playing? Play is a crucial part of a child's cognitive development and is fantastic for exploring senses, building creativity, and discovering how things work.

According to the American Academy of Pediatrics, play is important because it helps the mental, physical, and social well-being of a child. It's also a wonderful way for parents to engage with their children and encourage early learning.

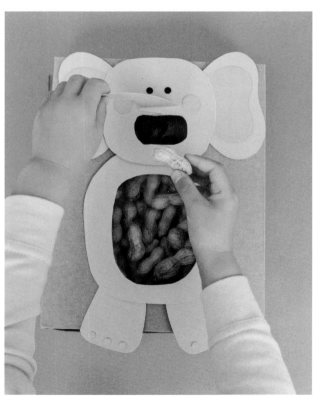

This book is about playing and learning with your kids. It's about having fun through creative process-oriented projects and not worrying about having the perfect craft material on hand. That's why you'll only find common recyclable household materials here such as paper tubes, cardboard, plastic bottles, egg cartons, and lids.

The Harvard Graduate School of Education notes that play comes in many different forms. There is social play with others, independent play during which kids make-believe or play with various toys, and guided play where children play in the context of a scene parents have set up. Although the projects here do have a guide toward a finished activity, we hope that our instructions are loosely guided tools for you to create, play, and learn with your child. Also, we invite you to set up invitations with the projects made by adding resources readily available at home to provide a richer learning experience. An example would be to make a box maze with a different configuration or provide sensory items like colored dyed rice or beans to our egg carton truck for additional play.

In this book, you'll find the focus is not on a finished craft but on the process of building a meaningful project with many learning iterations you can add on your own. We offer tips on how to extend play and learning for each project. But the possibilities are endless, so we encourage you to engage with your kids to come up with fun additions.

By using recyclable materials, we've also tried to keep this book accessible, low-cost, and no-waste so families can focus on creating and get started right away. Although we provide a framework for projects, they can be adjusted to your child's interest. Instead of a seal ball-and-cup paper tube game, why not create a shark if your child likes them better than seals?

I've combined my decade of experience as a mom and creative to bring you these unique and playful recycled projects. I know these activities will lead to precious bonding time with your kids but will create wonderful learning experiences, too. Happy playing and learning!

Find more playful, creative learning projects at **www.hellowonderful.co.**

SAFETY NOTE These projects are meant for parents to create to play and learn with their children. All activities require adult supervision. Parents or adults should be the only ones operating craft materials such as sharp scissors, craft knives, or hot glue guns.

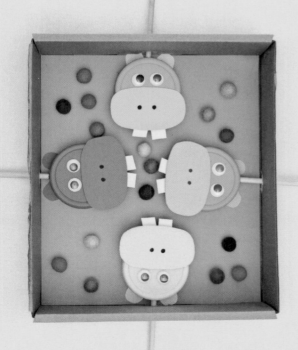

CHAPTER 1

FANTASTIC FOOD BOXES

▲▲▲▲▲▲

You'll never look at a cereal, snack, or pizza box the same after you see some of the fun activities in the next few pages. Create a fun bean toss game from a pizza box (page 18), transform a cereal box into a fun elephant feeding game (page 20), or relive your childhood with ravenous hippos (page 22). Make characters come alive, practice dexterity, and learn shapes all while having fun with boxes.

HELPFUL HINTS Remove your snack or cereal packages from their boxes when you get home from the grocery store and place the food items in reusable pantry bins or containers. This way, you can save lots of food boxes in a short amount of time and have them handy to craft when you need them.

Break up your food box so that it lays flat. Detach the sides of the box and re-form it inside out. Now, you have a plain box without any logos.

PIZZA BOX POMPOM MAZE

▲▲

Just when you thought that your leftover pizza box was making its way to the recycling bin, why not upcycle it at home instead? Turn the inside of the cardboard pizza box into an entertaining pompom maze. Create walls and a path to try to move the pompoms around the maze. This craft is super fun for kids, creative, and great for cognitive skills.

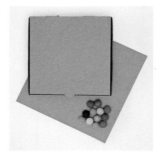

MATERIALS

A cardboard cutout that is the same size as the square pizza box

Craft knife

Craft glue or hot glue gun and hot glue sticks

Scrap cardboard

Paper tube

Small pizza box

Pompoms

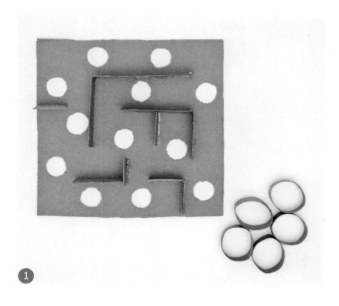

PROCEDURE

1 Cut holes in your piece of cardboard cutout and glue strips of cardboard in various places as shown to create a maze or block for the pompoms. Cut 5 small, equally sized stacks from your paper roll that will be tall enough to fit inside your pizza box to lift up the cutout.

2 Glue the paper tube stacks to the cutout and insert your cutout inside your pizza box.

HOW TO PLAY

Add pompoms on top of the maze and have kids move the box around to try to get the pompoms to drop inside the holes.

Learning Skills ▶ Fine motor skills, color recognition

Tips to Extend Play ▶ Instead of a maze shape, you can omit the cardboard barriers and have kids try to throw balls inside the holes for a fun ball game. You can make larger holes and get bigger pompoms to make it easier for younger children.

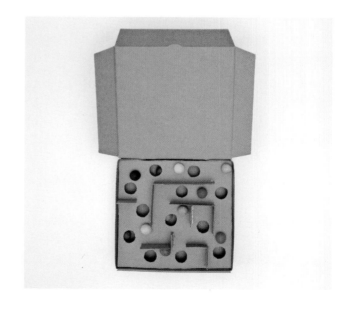

CARDBOARD BOX TV

Save the next empty food box that you have and turn it into a TV. Create an engaging puppet scene with this imaginative screen. Kids can help draw endless characters and themes to make their TV show come alive while they narrate story plots and twists.

MATERIALS

Craft knife

Scrap cardboard

Food box

Craft glue or hot glue gun and hot glue sticks

3 food pouch lids

Red and white cardstock

Paint sticks or crayons

Popsicle sticks

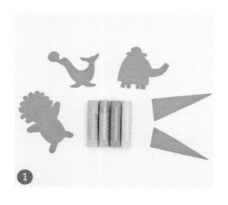 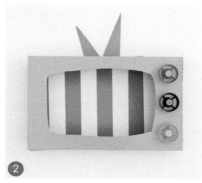 

PROCEDURE

1 Cut characters out of scrap cardboard. We did a circus theme and created a seal, elephant, and lion. Cut out cardboard TV antennas.

2 Cut an opening on the front of your food box. Glue the antennas, the pouch lids for "dials," and red and white paper to resemble a circus.

3 Paint or color your cardboard characters and glue them to popsicle sticks.

4 Cut 3 slits on top of the TV and insert the popsicle stick characters.

HOW TO PLAY

Move the sticks up and down like puppets to make the TV characters come alive.

Learning Skills ▸ Fine motor skills, imaginative play, creative skills

Tips to Extend Play ▸ Instead of a circus theme, create new learning themes (e.g., fruits and vegetables, ocean animals, vehicles). The possibilities are endless.

PIZZA BOX BEAN TOSS

▲▲▲▲▲▲▲▲▲▲▲▲▲▲▲▲▲▲▲▲▲▲▲▲▲▲▲▲▲▲▲▲▲▲

Kids love a good toss game, and learning shapes can be fun when you're throwing them in the air. In this case, there's a goal: Match up the right cardboard shape with the shape that's cut out in the box. This is a fun and interactive way to learn shapes and colors. If tossing is too hard, that's no problem. Your child can easily take the shapes one by one and put them directly into the matching shape holes, as well.

MATERIALS

Pizza box

Pencil

Craft knife

2 toilet paper tubes

Craft glue or hot glue gun and hot glue sticks

Scrap cardboard

Paint or paint sticks

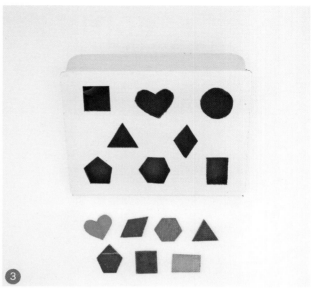

PROCEDURE

1   Draw shapes in pencil on top of your food box and then cut them out with a craft knife.

2   Open the box and glue on your 2 tubes to support it. Position the tubes on the side where the box opens so that the tubes angle the box's top.

3   Cut scrap cardboard into the same shapes you cut on the box and color with paint or paint sticks.

HOW TO PLAY

Have kids toss the cardboard shapes inside the right shape on the box for a fun toss game. Name the shapes and colors as they're tossed.

Learning Skills ▶ Shape and color recognition, cognitive skills

Tips to Extend Play ▶ Add numbers or letters to the shapes and call them out (e.g., "Can you put the 'B' in the circle?")

FEEDING ELEPHANT GAME

Save your empty cereal box and turn it into a hungry elephant instead. Kids will love feeding peanuts to the elephant. Since this project calls for transparent plastic, kids will get a kick out of seeing the elephant swallow the food and the peanuts lying in its stomach.

MATERIALS

Blue, pink, gray, and black paper

Scissors

Clear plastic (e.g., a clamshell clear food package, commonly used for baked goods)

Craft glue or hot glue gun and hot glue sticks

Food box

Peanuts

PROCEDURE

1   Cut your papers into a cute elephant shape that will fit your box.

2   Cut an opening for the mouth and belly on the box.

3   Cut an opening on the paper belly. Cut your clear plastic so that it fits on top of the belly and then glue those together.

4   Glue your elephant parts to the box. Only the mouth should have an opening.

HOW TO PLAY

Feed the elephant peanuts through the opening and count as you go.

Learning Skills ▸ Fine motor skills, counting

Tips to Extend Play ▸ Feed the elephant other small objects, such as colored items, cardboard shapes, letters, numbers, or sight words, for additional learning.

FOOD BOX HIPPO GAME

▲▲

Did you ever play the iconic Hungry Hungry Hippos game when you were a kid? It features four colorful hippos that retract their mouths to catch balls. You can make your own version with a food box. What's great is that you can utilize two recyclable materials here: lids and food boxes. Kids will love practicing their fine motor skills and maneuvering the sticks to try to catch pompoms.

MATERIALS

Scissors

Colored paper

Craft glue or hot glue gun and hot glue sticks

8 googly eyes

4 6" (15.2 cm) dowel sticks (or use any strong sticks you can find such as thick paper straws)

4 lids (use colored ones or paint your own)

Bottom of a food box

Craft knife

Colored cardstock for the base of the food box (optional)

Pompoms

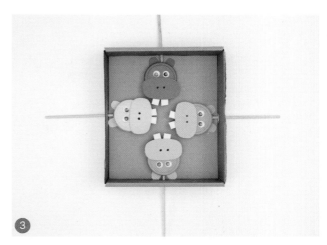

PROCEDURE

1   Make the hippo's face by adding details with paper that correspond to your lid color. We added an oval face, white teeth, and a nose. Glue the face parts and eyes to each lid.

2   Glue a dowel stick to each end of a lid.

3   Using the base of a food box, cut out 4 channels that you can fit your dowels through. Glue on colored cardstock as a base (optional) or leave the cardboard base blank.

HOW TO PLAY

Add pompoms to the center of the cardboard base and have your child try to catch the pompoms inside the lids. This can be played with up to four players. Name the color of the pompoms as you're catching them.

Learning Skills ▶ Fine motor skills, color recognition, cognitive skills

Tips to Extend Play ▶ Use various sized pompoms to see which ones are more challenging. What else can the hippo catch? Make small cardboard shapes and add numbers and letters to them.

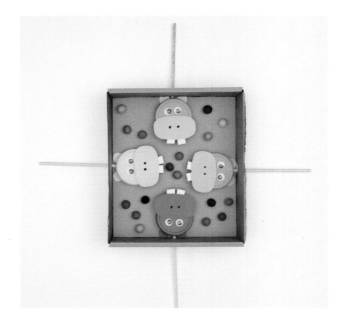

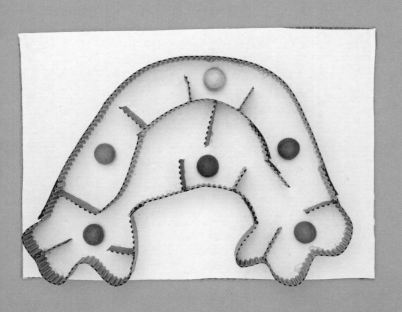

CHAPTER 2

CREATIVE CARDBOARD CREATIONS

▲▲▲▲▲▲

I think we can all agree cardboard is one of the most fun and versatile recyclable materials out there. Cardboard can be a blank canvas for creating anything you want and imagine. Making puzzles is one of our favorite ways to create with cardboard. Make it more challenging by tracing lines and shapes (page 26), incorporating early math (page 32), or talking to kids about emotions (page 34).

....

HELPFUL HINT When you need flat cardboard, just break down the sides of a box and stack them neatly in one pile. When you need them for fun projects, they will be easy to grab.

....

TRACING LINES AND SHAPES

Did you know that tracing lines and shapes is a precursor to writing? Have kids use their fingers to trace lines with this fun tracing activity. They will love running their fingers through the cardboard grooves to trace shapes for a fun, tactile sensory activity. The recessed grooves also make a great invitation to play by adding sensory items, such as dyed rice, to put inside.

MATERIALS

2 pieces of square cardboard

Pencil

Craft knife

Cardstock paper to fit the cardboard

Craft glue or hot glue gun and hot glue sticks

PROCEDURE

1 On 1 piece of cardboard, draw thick lines. We drew curves, zigzags, and square designs.

2 Use a craft knife on a cutting mat to cut out the lines.

3 Place a colored piece of paper over the second piece of flat cardboard, and then put the cut cardboard on top.

4 Glue the cardboard and paper in place or choose to leave them as is so you can switch out the colored paper underneath.

HOW TO PLAY

Encourage your child to use their fingers to trace over the lines.

Learning Skills ▸ Fine motor skills, sensory exploration, pre-writing exercise

Tips to Extend Play ▸ Place sensory items such as colored rice and shapes in the cut lines as a fun scooping and sensory activity.

....

NOTE If you choose not to glue down the cardboard, secure the sides with binder clips to prevent the top cardboard from sliding off.

....

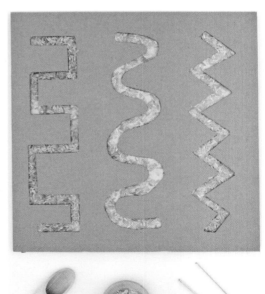

SHAPE SENSORY PUZZLE

▲▲▲▲▲▲▲▲▲▲▲▲▲▲▲▲▲▲▲▲▲▲▲▲▲▲▲▲▲▲▲▲▲▲▲▲

If you're looking for a fast and do-it-yourself way to have the kids work on learning their shapes, make shapes out of corrugated cardboard, then have the kids fill the inside of those shapes with rice. This is a simple and engaging way to learn while having some sensory fun.

MATERIALS

Corrugated cardboard

Craft glue or hot glue gun and hot glue sticks

Cardboard

Rice

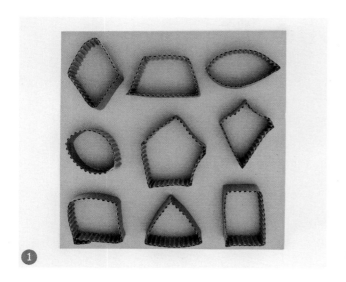

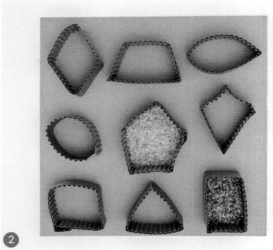

PROCEDURE

1 Bend your corrugated cardboard into shapes. Glue them onto your cardboard base.

2 Fill shapes with rice.

HOW TO PLAY

Scoop and fill shapes with rice. Call out shapes as you fill them up. If using colored rice like we did, you can also add some fun color learning.

Learning Skills ▸ Shape and color recognition, fine motor skills, sensory exploration

Tips to Extend Play ▸ Fill shapes with different sensory materials like pasta, beads, pompoms, or sand. Ask about the tactile feel of each. Or, instead of bending corrugated cardboard into shapes, create an animal—for example, a dinosaur, and add green rice or green pompoms inside.

RAINBOW CARDBOARD MAZE

Mazes offer cognitive fun. All you need to make this happy maze is some corrugated cardboard that you can mold into a rainbow shape. Then, just add colored pompoms and let the kids move them around. Will they be able to put the colors in order of how they appear on the rainbow? Challenge them to see if they can get it done.

MATERIALS

Pencil

Cardboard base

Scissors

Corrugated cardboard

Craft glue or hot glue gun and hot glue sticks

Pompoms

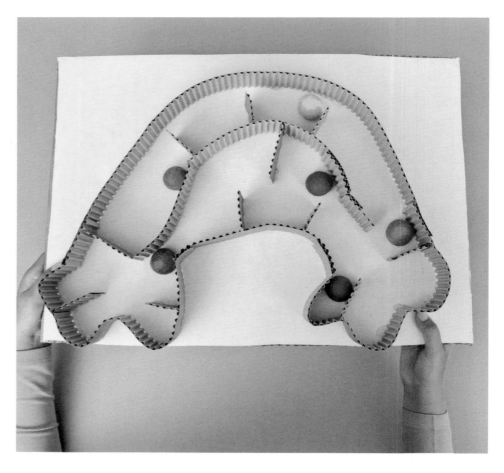

PROCEDURE

1 Draw a rainbow with 2 clouds on the flat cardboard base.

2 Cut strips of corrugated cardboard and glue along your penciled rainbow lines. Add stoppers inside the rainbow with strips of the cardboard.

3 Add pompoms inside the rainbow maze.

HOW TO PLAY

Move the pompoms around the maze to get through one end of the rainbow to another.

Learning Skills ▸ Fine motor skills, color recognition

Tips to Extend Play ▸ Instead of using the rainbow as a maze, use it as a sensory bin. Scoop sensory items, such as colored dyed rice, beans, or any small loose parts, inside the maze. Or arrange pompoms in rainbow order on the arches.

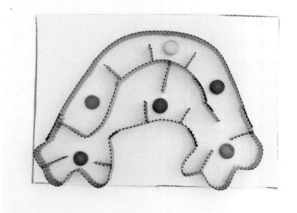

EARLY MATH POMPOM GAME

▲▲▲

Who says that math should be stressful and hard? This early math cardboard activity can teach kids simple equations and colors at the same time. This math board game can be simple yet is versatile enough to introduce more challenging numbers. The pompoms provide a visual and tactile way to count.

MATERIALS

2 pieces of equally sized flat cardboard

Craft knife ·

Craft glue or hot glue gun and hot glue sticks

Extra pieces of cardboard to make squares for numbers

Marker

Pompoms

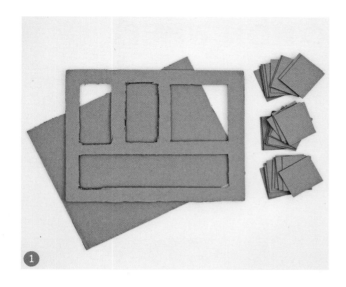

PROCEDURE

1 From 1 piece of cardboard, cut out 2 rectangles, 1 square, and a long skinny rectangle on the bottom that will fit 4 small square cutouts. Glue the cutout to the other large piece of cardboard. Cut out multiple small cardboard squares.

2 Write numbers and +, -, and = signs on 3 squares. Write numbers 1-9 on the other squares to incorporate simple math.

HOW TO PLAY

Insert numbers in the bottom rectangle with either the plus or minus sign and have your child add or subtract the right number of pompoms on the top squares.

Learning Skills ▸ Early math, counting, numbers, cognitive skills

Tips to Extend Play ▸ Go beyond the number 10 and use double digits. Or try simple multiplication. Coordinate the pompoms by color.

CARDBOARD EMOTION WHEEL

Do you want a fun and colorful way to talk to your child about emotions? When kids are small, big emotions can be hard to talk about. This is a great way to have them interact and be part of the discussion. They get to spin the wheel and land on an emotion each time. Have them act out that emotion as you talk about it and discuss how it feels.

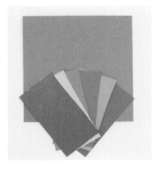

MATERIALS

2 pieces of cardboard

Craft knife

Cardstock in colors of the rainbow (red, orange, yellow, green, blue, purple)

Black marker

Craft glue or hot glue gun and hot glue sticks

Brad

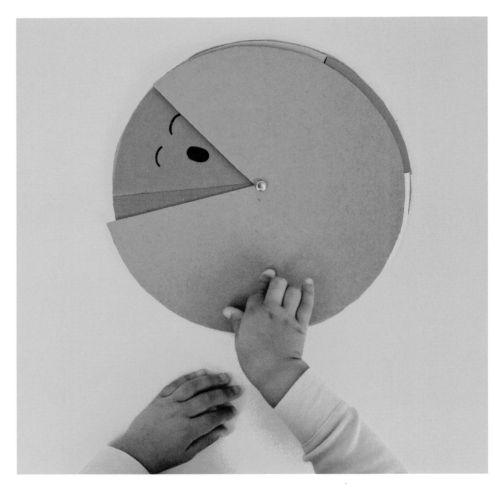

RECYCLE AND PLAY

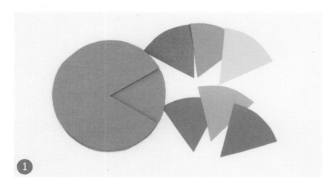

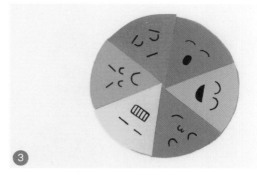

PROCEDURE

1 Cut 2 matching circles from the 2 pieces of cardboard. Equally divide one into 6 and cut out a triangle. Use that as a template to cut 6 pieces of paper, 1 piece per color.

2 Draw different face emotions on each paper triangle.

3 Glue the paper triangles to the cardboard circle.

4 Lay the cardboard with the triangle cutout over the circles with faces and cut a hole in the center to insert your brad. Now your wheel can spin.

HOW TO PLAY

Turn the wheel and identity emotions and colors. Talk about how each emotion feels with your kids (sad, happy, surprised, angry, etc.).

Learning Skills ▶ Color recognition, cognitive and social developmental skills

Tips to Extend Play ▶ Instead of faces, you can draw animals, plants, flowers, or any type of learning theme to learn more about that subject.

CHAPTER 3

PLAYFUL PAPER TUBE PROJECTS

▲▲▲▲▲▲

When I think of the most versatile recycled material to craft with, paper tubes make the top of my list. My kids would agree, too. With the humble paper tube, we can make one of our favorite animals and practice learning colors and threading (page 38). We can zoom around with our cars in our paper tube garage (page 40) or hone our cutting skills by creating crazy haircuts (page 44).

....

HELPFUL HINT We like to stack our paper tubes inside a box right-side up so they are easy to sort by shape. This way, they won't get squished and are easy to grab.

....

PAPER TUBE CATERPILLAR THREADING

Caterpillars are a favorite preschool bug. This rainbow caterpillar can teach kids colors and also makes a fun and easy yarn activity. The shapes of the tubes are large enough so that yarn can easily go through. Kids can focus on learning the motion and movement of how to thread from one tube to another while practicing their fine motor skills.

MATERIALS

3 toilet paper tubes, cut in half

Colored paper in red, orange, yellow, green, blue, and purple

Craft glue or hot glue gun and hot glue sticks

1 12" (30.5 cm) cardboard square

1 green pipe cleaner

2 small yellow pompoms

2 googly eyes

Yarn

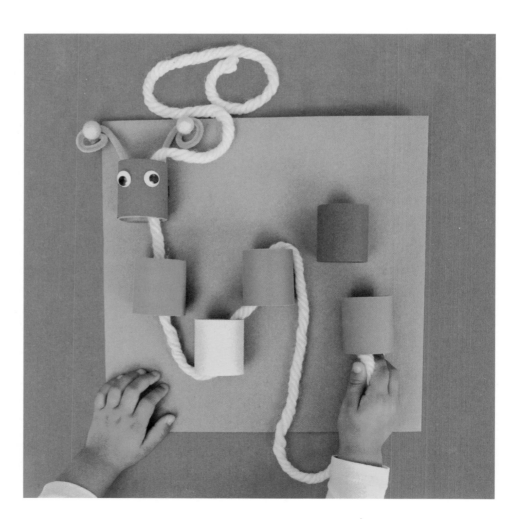

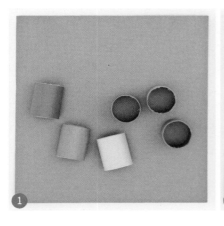
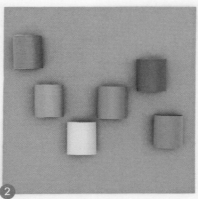
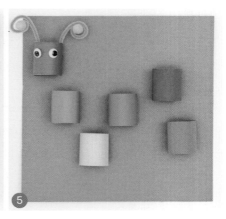

PROCEDURE

1 Cut your colored paper to fit around your tubes and secure them with glue.

2 Arrange them in rainbow order (red, orange, yellow, green, blue, purple) on top of your cardboard. Lay them out so they resemble a caterpillar shape. Glue down the tubes to keep them from moving.

3 Bend your pipe cleaner in half, curl the ends, and glue the pieces to the red tube as antennas. Curl the tops.

4 Glue the 2 yellow pompoms on top of the pipe cleaners.

5 Glue the 2 googly eyes on the red tube.

HOW TO PLAY

Have your child practice fine motor skills by threading yarn through the tubes. Point out the colors on the caterpillar's body and name them.

Learning Skills ▸ Fine motor skills, color recognition

Tips to Extend Play ▸ Add letters or numbers on the caterpillar tubes for additional learning. You can simply write letters on strips of paper and attach them using removable tape.

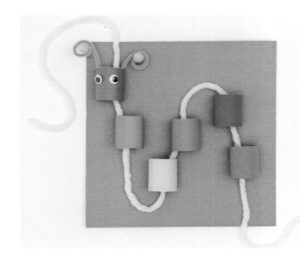

CAR GARAGE AND RAMP

Save those empty tubes and make the coolest ramp and toy car storage activity. The kids' favorite toy cars will fit perfectly in the tubes, and the kids will be able to pull them out and play with them on the fun ramp, too. The colored tubes also introduce color learning.

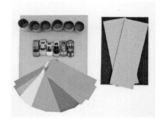

MATERIALS

10 toilet paper tubes, cut in half

Colored cardstock

Craft knife

Black cardstock

White crayon

Flat piece of cardboard plus another piece for the ramp and stand

Craft glue or hot glue gun and hot glue sticks

Toy cars

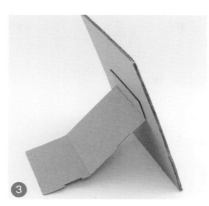
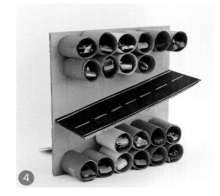

PROCEDURE

1 Wrap your paper tubes in colored cardstock.

2 Cut a piece of black paper that will fit over your ramp and add road lines with a white crayon. Glue that over your ramp.

3 Glue another piece of cardboard to the flat cardboard to create a stand.

4 Glue your tubes and ramps as shown.

HOW TO PLAY

Move cars inside the paper tube garage and down the ramp. Match colored cars to the garage color. Call out the car's color as it goes down the ramp.

Learning Skills ▸ Fine motor skills, creative play, color recognition

Tips to Extend Play ▸ Add dot stickers to the cars and top the paper tubes with corresponding words or letters to match. Learn some math by adding and subtracting cars from the paper tube garage.

SEAL BALL-AND-CUP GAME

This seal ball-and-cup activity is a fun variation on a classic game. This is very much like the iconic ball-and-cup game from back in the day, but the addition of a seal adds a playful touch. This is a fine motor activity for the kids that does a great job at having them work on their focus, concentration, accuracy, and hand-eye coordination. And just know that this is harder than it looks, in case you want to give it a try.

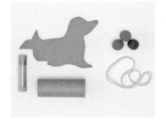

MATERIALS

Cardboard

Scissors

Silver paint or paint stick

Black marker

Craft glue or hot glue gun and hot glue sticks

Paper tube

Yarn or string

Pompom

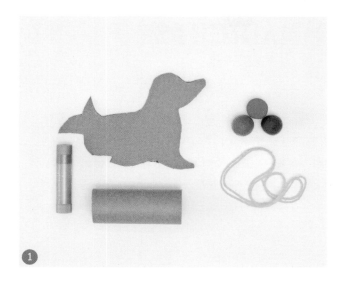

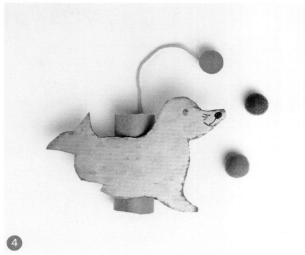

PROCEDURE

1 Cut your cardboard into a seal shape.

2 Paint the seal silver and add face details with the black marker.

3 Glue the seal to the paper tube.

4 Glue your string to the inside of your paper tube and attach a pompom on the opposite end.

HOW TO PLAY

Try to catch the pompom inside the paper tube. What happens if you use a shorter or longer string? Is it easier or more challenging?

Learning Skills ▸ Fine motor skills

Tips to Extend Play ▸ If the string is too challenging, you can simply set the tube down and ask kids to stuff the tube with pompoms. Call out colors or count as you go.

CRAZY PAPER HAIRCUTS

Doesn't every kid want to practice cutting hair? This paper tube haircut activity gives them that chance while they also work on their fine motor skills. Using leftover paper tubes is a great way to upcycle products in your home, and adding on the paper strips for the kids to cut is a fun perk. This simple activity will help kids work on hand-eye coordination in a fun and relatable way. After all, everyone needs a haircut at some point.

MATERIALS

Paper tubes

Scissors

Colored cardstock

Tape, craft glue, or hot glue gun and hot glue sticks

White cardstock

Black marker

PROCEDURE

1 Cut cardstock into rectangles that will wrap around the top of your tube. This will be the hair. Then cut strips down the middle in various shapes. You can make crinkle shapes, curl the strips, or just leave them straight.

2 Cover your paper tube with colored cardstock. Secure with tape or glue.

3 Add your hair over the paper tubes and secure with tape or glue. Make small eyes with white paper and black markers and glue the features onto the tubes.

HOW TO PLAY

Provide child-safe scissors and ask your child to cut the strips of hair to give the paper tubes haircuts.

Learning Skills ▸ Fine motor skills, color recognition

Tips to Extend Play ▸ Ask your child what color the tubes and hair are. Count the strips they cut and add or subtract them.

PAPER TUBE SHAPE STAMPING

Kids love learning various shapes. This creative paper tube shape stamping adds some art and creativity to learning shapes. Save those paper rolls and use them for this fun stamping activity. Just fold the ends into a shape and dip them in paint. The kids can then use them to create designs, wrapping paper, cards, and fun pictures.

MATERIALS

Paper tubes

Paint

Paper

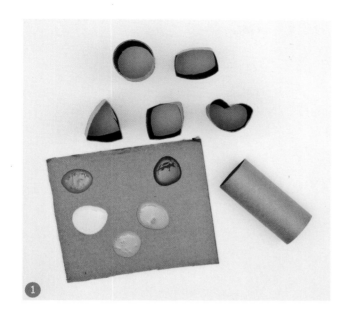

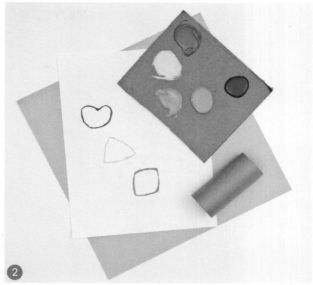

PROCEDURE

1 Manipulate paper tube ends into shapes such as a heart, square, rectangle, triangle. Leave 1 as is for a circle.

2 Dip the tubes in paint and stamp shapes onto paper.

HOW TO PLAY

Call out shapes and colors as they are stamped on the paper.

Learning Skills ▸ Art, shapes, colors, creative skills

Tips to Extend Play ▸ Stamp shapes in a line and count them to add them up.

CHAPTER 4

BEST BUBBLE WRAP PLAY

▲▲▲▲▲▲

Bubble wrap is one of the most fun and tactile recycled items to create with. Kids are naturally drawn to the squishy bubbles and the fun texture. And who doesn't love popping bubble wrap? Its unique sensory feel makes it an ideal material for creating a beautiful mess-free painting (page 50), doing stamping activities such as our bubble wrap animals (pages 52 and 56), or making clothespin butterflies for textured wings and numbers (page 58).

....

HELPFUL HINT To store bubble wrap, separate the ones that are still intact from the ones that are deflated. Gently roll the bubble wrap a few sheets as you get them and secure with a rubber band so they can store lightly without getting damaged.

....

MESS-FREE BUBBLE WRAP PAINTING

The kids might think this bubble wrap painting activity is magic because they're not going to understand how they're *not* making a mess. But the secret to creating this mess-free craft is to put the bubble wrap *over* the paint and then let the kids have fun squishing the paint through the bubble wrap. They'll love all the sensory feels that they're getting while creating a truly unique work of art.

MATERIALS

White cardstock

Paints in various colors

Bubble wrap

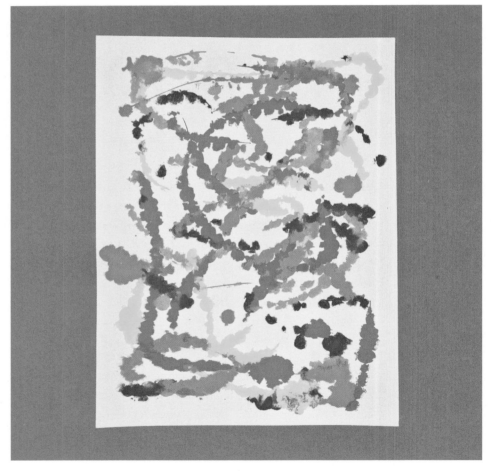

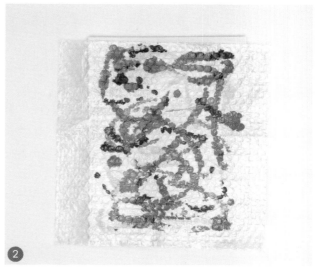

PROCEDURE

1 Splatter paint over white cardstock. You can use a canvas, watercolor paper, or even cardboard instead.

2 Press a piece of bubble wrap over your selected canvas and have your kids smoosh the paint around.

HOW TO PLAY

After squishing the paint around, remove the bubble wrap to reveal a piece of beautiful abstract art. You can make another print with the bubble wrap by pressing it onto another piece of paper.

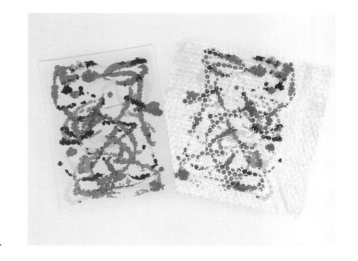

Learning Skills ▶ Art, sensory exploration, creative skills, color recognition

Tips to Extend Play ▶ For older kids, use a paint brush and paint directly on the bubble wrap to make fun prints that are more directed in colors and patterns.

WHALE BUBBLE WRAP ART

▲▲▲▲▲▲▲▲▲▲▲▲▲▲▲▲▲▲▲▲▲▲▲▲▲▲▲▲▲▲▲▲▲▲▲

There is so much that you can do creatively with bubble wrap. This bubble wrap whale is proof of that. Have the kids draw a whale on the bubble wrap with a black sharpie and then use blue paint to color it in. Once they press it down on white paper, it'll transfer the image, and they'll have quite the "whale of a tale" to show you!

MATERIALS

Black marker

Bubble wrap

Blue paint and paint brush

Black and white cardstock

Scissors

Craft glue or hot glue gun and hot glue sticks

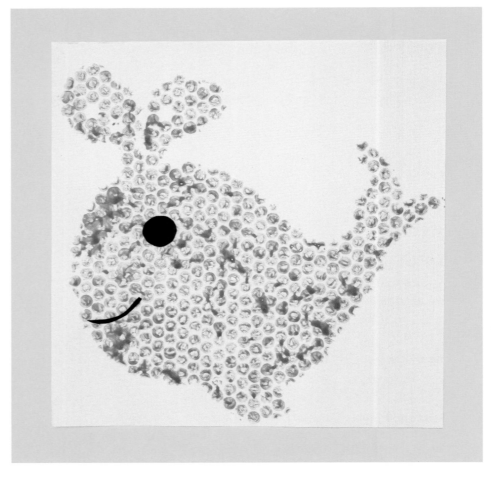

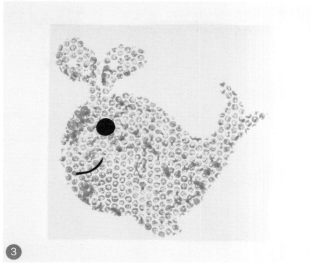

PROCEDURE

1 Draw a whale shape on bubble wrap and paint it blue.

2 Cut out an eye and smile from black cardstock.

3 Transfer the whale image (paint side down) onto your white cardstock. Glue on the smile and eye.

HOW TO PLAY

Lift up the bubble wrap to reveal a magical image print! Kids will love seeing the tiny bubbles come into life as a whale painting.

Learning Skills ▶ Fine motor skills, art, scissor and cutting skills

Tips to Extend Play ▶ You can create any shape, animal, or object you want by just drawing on the bubble wrap with a marker and painting it any color you want.

ICE CREAM STAMPING AND COUNTING

You scream, I scream, we all scream for ice cream! This fun ice cream stamping is a sweet way to recycle bubble wrap to create colorful and delicious ice cream cones. When combined with the paint, the cardboard cones and the bubble wrap create a fun texture and effect. Kids can focus on combining colors, counting the scoops, and working on their creative skills, as well.

MATERIALS

Scissors

Cardboard

Tape, craft glue, or hot glue gun and hot glue sticks

Bubble wrap

Paper tube

Rubber band

Paint

Paper

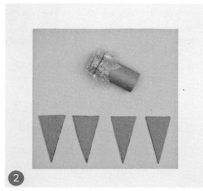

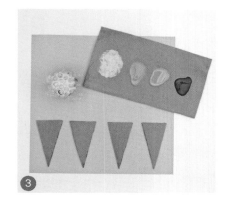

PROCEDURE

1 Cut cardboard into cone shapes.

2 Tape or glue your cones onto a piece of a paper. Wrap a piece of bubble wrap over your paper tube (bubble-side up) and secure with a rubber band.

3 Pour paint onto a piece of paper. Dip bubble wrap onto paint so there is a think, even coat and stamp scoops of ice cream. Replace bubble wrap for different colors.

HOW TO PLAY

Count the number of scoops and add them up.

Learning Skills ▶ Art, fine motor skills, counting, color recognition, sensory exploration

Tips to Extend Play ▶ Stamp scoops by color and name them.

BUBBLE WRAP LION

▲▲▲▲▲▲▲▲▲▲▲▲▲▲▲▲▲▲▲▲▲▲▲▲▲▲▲▲▲▲▲▲

Don't miss this fun bubble wrap lion craft. This is another excellent way to use bubble wrap to create a fiercely loved animal with the kids. Grab colored paint and let the kids have fun painting the bubbles on the wrap. Adding on strips of orange hair creates a fun scissor skills activity. There's nothing scary about this bubble wrap lion.

MATERIALS

Bubble wrap

Yellow paint

Paint brush

Craft glue or hot glue gun and hot glue sticks

Black, orange, yellow, and white cardstock

Scissors

Pencil

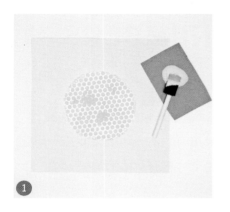

PROCEDURE

1 Cut a circle out of the bubble wrap and paint the wrap yellow. Once dried, glue the wrap on top of white cardstock.

2 Cut out your lion face and features. Cut strips of orange for the hair.

3 Glue the features to the bubble wrap face.

4 Use a pencil to curl the paper strips.

HOW TO PLAY

Practice fine motor skills by curling the lion's mane and snipping it.

Learning Skills ▸ Fine motor skills, art, scissor and cutting skills

Tips to Extend Play ▸ Make a rainbow lion's mane and call out the strips by color. Create other animals with the same method. Think of animals with "hair," such as a unicorn with a rainbow mane.

CLOTHESPIN BUTTERFLY NUMBERS

Butterflies are loved by many for their beautiful wings. This bubble wrap butterfly activity will have the kids counting, using their fine motor skills, and creating beautiful homemade butterflies with clothespins. This activity is all about creativity and working on number recognition, and it's also a fun matching game.

MATERIALS

Cardboard

Scissors

Bubble wrap

Clothespins

Craft glue or hot glue gun and hot glue sticks

Googly eyes

Pipe cleaners

Removable dot stickers

Marker

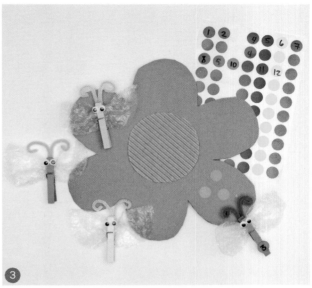

PROCEDURE

1 Cut your cardboard into a flower shape.

2 Make clothespin butterflies by adding a semi-circle of bubble wrap between the clothespin. This will create the wings. Glue on eyes and pipe cleaner antennas.

3 Add dot stickers to each petal. Write a number on 1 dot sticker to place on each clothespin butterfly.

HOW TO PLAY

Match the dot sticker number on each butterfly to the number of dots on each petal.

Learning Skills ▸ Fine motor skills, color recognition, numbers, counting, sensory exploration

Tips to Extend Play ▸ Match the colored dot to the same color on the petal. Instead of numbers, use letters or match lowercase to uppercase letters.

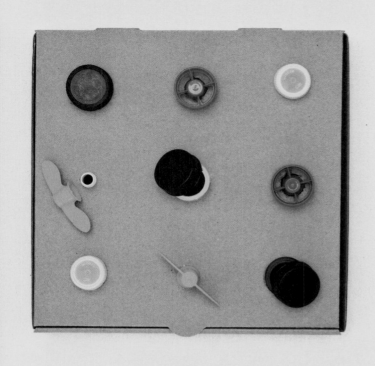

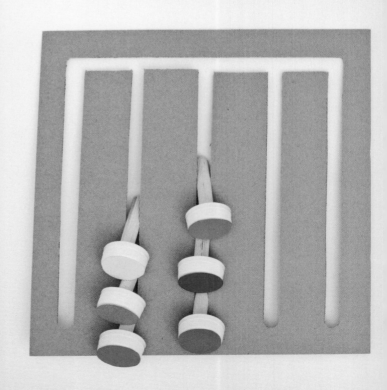

CHAPTER 5

CAPTIVATING LID AND CAP ACTIVITIES

▲▲▲▲▲▲▲

We are a household overflowing with lids, and if you have young kids, you can relate. Food pouch lids are some of the most recognizable ones in many homes with young children. Save those lids and learn the alphabet by adding lid letters on top of a rainbow (page 68) or transform them into amazing bottle cap mazes (page 70). Screwing lids on and off is also a fantastic fine motor activity for little kids (page 64).

....

HELPFUL HINT Lids can be sorted by size or color to easily grab, and they can be stored inside recycled food or Mason jars to keep secure and save them from toppling over.

....

TURTLE LID ANIMAL COUNTING

How many lids do you have just lying around the house? Don't let them go to waste. Use them for this fun turtle activity instead. Turn the lids into turtle shells that are bright and colorful. Then, add on the colored dots to help the kids match up the colors and also work on their counting skills. Slow and steady is a good mantra when working with the kids on counting.

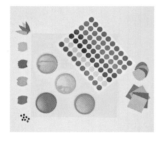

MATERIALS

Colored lids (or you can paint your own lids)

Colored cardstock that coordinates with the lid colors

Craft glue or hot glue gun and hot glue sticks

Googly eyes

Marker

Removable dot stickers

PROCEDURE

1 Create a face, 4 flippers, and 1 tail per turtle using the same colored paper as your lid color. Glue the features to the turtle. Glue on the googly eyes.

2 Write numbers on small pieces of paper.

HOW TO PLAY

Place the right number of dot stickers that is on the piece of paper on the turtle.

Learning Skills ▸ Early math, numbers, color recognition

Tips to Extend Play ▸ You can write letters or numbers on the dot sticker. Place them on the turtles and simply ask your child to identify the right letter as you call them out.

BUSY BOARD LID ACTIVITY

Working on fine motor skills with the kids is important, so doing it in a fun way is key. This is why this box lids activity is perfect. All you need are a few different types of lids. Have the kids work on holding and screwing them down into the box. As their hands turn the lids on the opening, they will feel how the screws and lids work, fine-tuning their hand muscles.

MATERIALS

Box

Lids and caps with the bottom portions cut off

Craft knife

Craft glue or hot glue gun and hot glue sticks

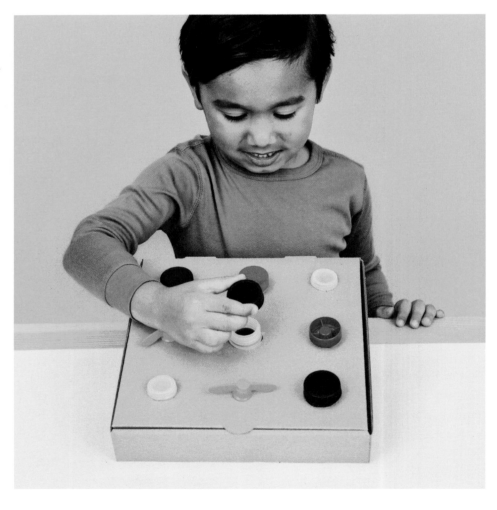

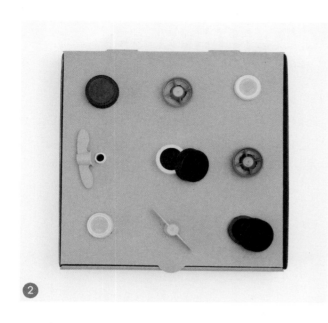

PROCEDURE

1 Determine where you will place your lids and create a hole large enough to fit the bottom cut-off portion through the hole.

2 Glue the bottom portion around the hole. Once you close your box, you should be able to match the lids to the bottoms and screw them on.

HOW TO PLAY

Match the right lids to the bottoms and screw them on the box.

Learning Skills ▸ Fine motor skills, cognitive skills

Tips to Extend Play ▸ Call out lid colors to practice color recognition. What else can you add to the box to practice fine motor skills? What about learning how to tie knots with string or gluing on various tactile items to create a sensory busy board?

LADYBUG LID COUNTING

Not only are ladybugs super fun to create, they're great for working on counting skills, too. Once the kids create this adorable cardboard ladybug using lids, they'll get to focus on counting and adding the pompom dots. This is a great way to work on number recognition and counting.

MATERIALS

Pencil

Cardboard

Black and red paints or paint sticks

Black and red pipe cleaners

Scissors

Craft glue or hot glue gun and hot glue sticks

Black lids

Red pompoms

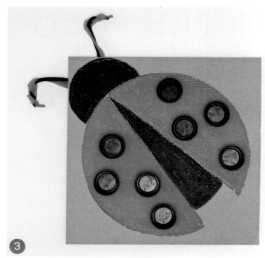

PROCEDURE

1 Draw a ladybug on your cardboard and then color it using your red and black paints or paint sticks.

2 Twist your black and red pipe cleaners together to make antennas, cut them to your desired size, and glue them to the cardboard ladybug.

3 Add lids on top of either of the ladybug's wings.

HOW TO PLAY

Drop the pompoms inside the lids. You can play various math games by counting lids and/or the pompoms. You can take away lids and ask your child to add a certain number on the ladybug.

Learning Skills ▶ Fine motor skills, early math, numbers, counting

Tips to Extend Play ▶ Add letters or numbers inside the lids instead of pompoms. Use small tongs and practice fine motor skills by picking up pompoms from one lid to another.

RAINBOW SHOOTING STAR ALPHABET

▲▲▲▲▲▲▲▲▲▲▲▲▲▲▲▲▲▲▲▲▲▲▲▲▲▲▲▲▲▲

Have you and the kids ever stepped outside at night and tried to see any shooting stars? If you're patient enough, you just might have seen a few. But if not, don't worry. Just grab up simple recycled materials such as bottle caps and let the kids create their very own rainbow shooting star. It's full of colors, super bright, and a beautiful art activity.

MATERIALS

Glitter paper

Scissors

Craft glue or hot glue gun and hot glue sticks

White cardstock

Paint sticks or markers in rainbow colors (red, orange, yellow, green, blue, purple)

26 bottle caps

Black marker

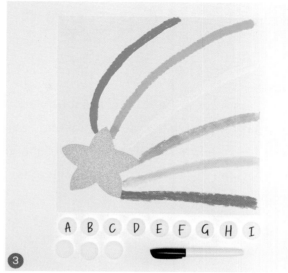

PROCEDURE

1 Cut a star shape out of glitter paper. Glue the star to your white cardstock.

2 Draw colored lines representing a rainbow shooting out of the star.

3 Write each letter of the alphabet on 26 caps.

HOW TO PLAY

Line up the caps in alphabetical order on the rainbow lines.

Learning Skills ▸ Letters and the alphabet

Tips to Extend Play ▸ Instead of letters, you can write numbers. For early math, you can also make a +, –, and = bottle cap and do simple math equations on the rainbow. Or add dot sticks on top of the lid and match the coordinating rainbow line.

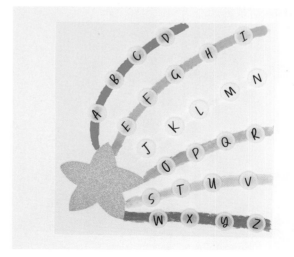

BOTTLE CAP MAZE

▲▲▲

Mazes are always a great idea. Preschoolers and early learners love to solve problems, too. Covering used caps with colored paper and using a simple dowel rod on the opposite side gives the kids the freedom to move the lids around and match them up with the colors. This is a great activity for learning colors and enhancing fine motor skills.

MATERIALS

1 12" (30.5 cm) cardboard square

Craft knife

Scissors

Craft glue or hot glue gun and hot glue sticks

Colored paper

3" (7.6 cm) dowel sticks, at least 4 per cap color

Plastic caps

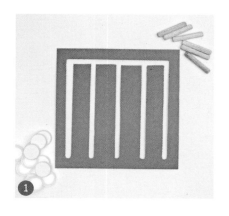

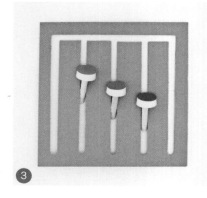

PROCEDURE

1 Cut 1 horizontal line on the top of the cardboard. Draw and cut 5 vertical lines coming down from the top line.

2 Glue colored paper on top of your caps. Glue the dowel sticks on the bottom side of the caps.

3 Insert the caps in the cardboard openings.

HOW TO PLAY

The object of the game is to move the caps by holding the dowel stick behind the cardboard and sorting the caps by color.

Learning Skills ▸ Fine motor skills, color recognition, cognitive skills

Tips to Extend Play ▸ Add letters to the bottle caps and try to spell out simple words or sight words.

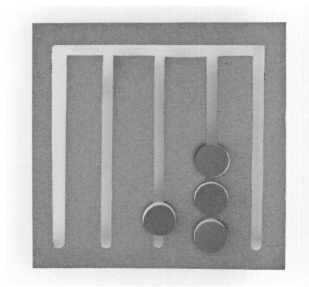

CHAPTER 6

BREATHTAKING BOTTLE IDEAS

▲▲▲▲▲▲

Many people toss a bottle into the recycling bin, but we see endless creative possibilities with them. Bottles are empty containers waiting to turn into the most playful characters, like our unicorn bottle (page 76). They can be stuffed to pretend-feed pigs (page 74). Or they can become a fun vehicle for games such as a pompom launcher, which helps children practice the push and pull motions.

HELPFUL HINT Hot, soapy water and some hard scrubbing will usually remove labels from jars. For sticky spots and residue, you can try using acetone or nail polish remover. You can also submerge your bottle or jar in hot water, dish soap, and vinegar for several minutes and then scrub off the label.

FEED THE PIG GAME

▲▲▲▲▲▲▲▲▲▲▲▲▲▲▲▲▲▲▲▲▲▲▲▲▲▲▲▲▲▲▲▲▲▲▲▲▲▲▲

This feed the pig activity is perfect for working on fine motor skills. Since we all know that pigs love to eat, the kids will have a blast stuffing pompoms right into this piggy's bottle belly. This activity will work on color recognition as well as fine-tuning grasping skills by picking up pompoms. And once the pig's tummy gets full, it's time to empty out and start all over again.

MATERIALS

Cardboard

Pencil

Pink paint or paint stick

Black marker

Craft knife

Large plastic bottle

Craft glue or hot glue gun and hot glue sticks

Pompoms

PROCEDURE

1 Draw a pig on your cardboard with a pencil. Color the pig with pink paint or a paint stick. Outline face details with a black marker.

2 Cut your bottle to about a ⅓ of its size from the narrow opening and hot glue the larger end to the middle of the pig.

HOW TO PLAY

Stuff the bottle with pompoms to feed the pig.

Learning Skills ▸ Fine motor skills, color recognition, sensory exploration

Tips to Extend Play ▸ What else can you stuff the pig with? Can you find some other objects that are different in sensory touch, such as rice or pasta? Or include some early math and add the right number of pompoms inside the bottle.

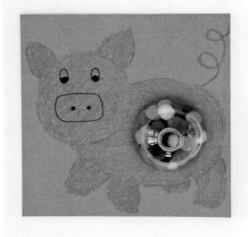

UNICORN BOTTLE GAME

▲▲

Unicorn rainbow hair, don't care! This recycled bottle activity is the perfect way to have the kids create an adorable unicorn full of soft and fluffy cotton balls. This can be a fun addition to their room or bathroom and an easy container to hold necessary supplies. Don't forget to add the rainbow hair and have the kids work on giving their unicorn a haircut to practice cutting skills.

MATERIALS

Black marker

Clean, empty bottle

Scissors

Gold glitter cardstock

Pink cardstock

Craft glue or hot glue gun
and hot glue sticks

Yarn in various colors

White cotton balls

PROCEDURE

1 Draw 2 sleepy eyes on the bottle with your black marker.

2 Cut out a gold horn and pink tail. Glue those on to the bottle.

3 Cut your yarn into strips that will flow about half the length down your bottle and glue them on the bottle.

HOW TO PLAY

Stuff the unicorn with the cotton balls.

Learning Skills ▸ Fine motor skills

Tips to Extend Play ▸ Cut the unicorn yarn hair and practice cutting skills. Add different colored pompoms for color recognition.

AQUARIUM SENSORY BOTTLE

▲▲▲▲▲▲▲▲▲▲▲▲▲▲▲▲▲▲▲▲▲▲▲▲▲▲▲▲▲▲▲▲▲▲▲▲

This aquarium bottle is a fun sensory activity for kids. It's as simple as adding baby oil and water to the bottle and filling it full of colorful ocean creations. Cut out cardboard fish and let the kids color or paint them, whichever they prefer. Once they've finished, just laminate with tape and let the fish float and swim in the water. With a little bit of help from paper clips, a magnet, and a popsicle stick, the kids can even try to go fishing.

MATERIALS

Pencil

Cardboard

Scissors

Markers, crayons, paint, or paint sticks

Clear packing tape

Paperclips

Baby oil

Dowel stick long enough to reach your paperclips

Craft glue or hot glue gun and hot glue sticks

Strong magnet

Piece of felt to cover the magnet

PROCEDURE

1 Draw simple fish shapes on cardboard and cut them out.

2 Color the fish with either markers, crayons, paint, or paint sticks, whichever you have on hand.

3 Add a strip of packing tape on the front and back of your fish and cut off the excess tape. Your cardboard fish is now "waterproof."

4 Clip 1 paperclip to each fish.

5 Add water and baby oil in a ratio of 3:1, respectively, inside your bottle.

6 Add your fish inside the bottle.

7 Take your dowel stick and glue your strong magnet onto it. Cover the magnet with a piece of felt to make it more secure so kids won't handle the magnet.

HOW TO PLAY

Use the magnetic fishing wand you created to pull the paper clip on the fish and use your fine motor skills to move them up and down the inside of the bottle.

Learning Skills ▸ Color recognition, fine motor skills

BALLOON POMPOM LAUNCHER

This awesome balloon pompom launcher makes good use out of a plastic bottle. Kids will love pulling the balloon end to make the pompoms fly. And don't worry; these soft balls won't hurt and are loads of fun to collect and count afterwards. This is a fantastic way to practice fine motor skills and learn colors.

MATERIALS

A clear plastic bottle, cleaned and dried

Scissors

Craft knife

1 balloon

Rubber bands

Small pompoms

PROCEDURE

1 Cut your bottle, leaving the bottle cap end intact with about a third of bottle still remaining.

2 Cut the tip off the top of the balloon. Cover the bottle opening with the balloon and secure with a few rubber bands. Knot your balloon.

HOW TO PLAY

Insert a few pompoms in the opening of the bottle and pull back the knotted balloon end to make the pompoms fly. Name colors of the pompoms as they launch out.

Learning Skills ▸ Fine motor skills, numbers, colors recognition

Tips to Extend Play ▸ Make it a fun game and ask your child how far the pompoms can go. Does pulling slower or faster make any difference? Measure the distance the pompoms reach.

FLOWER JAR PLANTERS

▲▲▲▲▲▲▲▲▲▲▲▲▲▲▲▲▲▲▲▲▲▲▲▲▲▲▲▲▲▲▲▲▲▲▲▲▲▲

Use leftover jars to make fun flowerpots. With soil that is actually dried black beans, this turns into a great sensory activity as well because the kids scoop the jars full. Cut out and add some colorful paper flowers and decorate the house with beautiful plants that will last forever. This is an easy project that can be done with flowers from every season.

MATERIALS

Various colored cardstock

Scissors

Craft glue or hot glue gun and hot glue sticks

Popsicle sticks

Jars or bottles

Black beans

PROCEDURE

1 Cut cardstock into flower shapes. Glue onto popsicle sticks.

2 Add black beans inside the jars and then add the flowers.

HOW TO PLAY

Scoop black beans inside jars and "plant" flowers.

Learning Skills ▸ Sensory exploration, fine motor skills, color recognition, planting and flower learning

Tips to Extend Play ▸ What else can you plant other than flowers? Try different fruits and vegetables. You can also try using real soil and planting herbs or succulents, which are easy beginner plants for kids.

J I B C G
F
D H P
C A

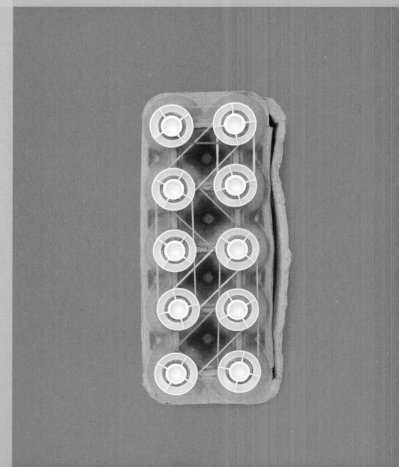

CHAPTER 7

EGG-CITING EGG CARTONS PROJECTS

▲▲▲▲▲▲

Egg cartons are truly "egg-citing" because they are the most surprising of all the commonly used recyclable materials. The material is firm, so it can be painted like our alligator letter feed (page 86) and veggie and fruit garden color sort (page 88). But is also soft, so it can be cut to create awesome toys like our sensory dump truck (page 92).

....

HELPFUL HINTS Watch your egg cartons for broken shell pieces or accidental egg leaks. You should remove them by cutting off those pieces before using egg cartons for crafting.

Stack egg cartons to save space.

Most egg cartons are easy to cut and absorb paint well because they are made of molded pulp and recycled paper.

....

ALLIGATOR LETTER FEED

Who knew that leftover egg cartons look just like alligators? Just paint the carton green and you'll see it for yourself. The kids will love feeding the alligator matching letters of the alphabet in their lowercase and uppercase forms. See if they're able to feed the alligator the whole alphabet before he gets too full.

MATERIALS

Egg carton plus 2 additional egg carton cups for the eyes

2 toilet paper tubes, cut into 4 pieces

Green paint

Scissors

Black, white, and yellow cardstock

Craft glue or hot glue gun and hot glue sticks

Black marker

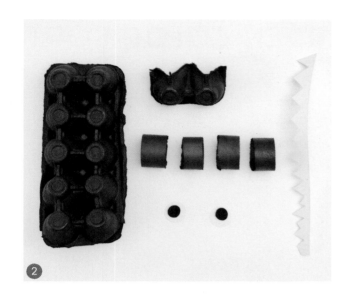

PROCEDURE

1 Paint the egg carton, 2 egg carton cups, and paper tubes green.

2 Create paper teeth and 2 eyes with white and black paper.

3 To assemble your alligator, glue the 2 egg carton cups on top of the full carton and glue on the eyes. Separate the bottom part of the container to create a mouth and glue on the paper teeth.

4 Write lower- and uppercase letters on yellow paper with a black marker (can be any other color as well).

HOW TO PLAY

Feed the alligator letters and call them out as you are feeding him. Match up lower- and uppercase letters and feed them as pairs.

Learning Skills ▸ Letter recognition, fine motor skills

Tips to Extend Play ▸ Introduce other learning elements by feeding the alligator shapes, numbers, or other sensory items.

VEGGIE AND FRUIT GARDEN COLOR SORT

Gardening and planting is a great hands-on activity for kids to learn at a young age. It's also a fantastic way to encourage kids to eat healthy fruits and vegetables by talking about all the various produce options out there. We love this veggie and fruit garden color sort because it teaches kids so many skills and is an engaging way to learn colors.

MATERIALS

12-count egg carton

Acrylic paint in rainbow colors (red, orange, yellow, green, blue, purple)

Scissors

Additional egg carton to cut out produce

Colored markers

Craft glue or hot glue gun and hot glue sticks

Colored popsicle sticks (or paint plain ones)

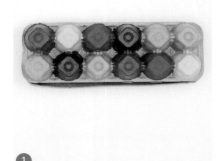 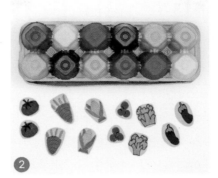 

PROCEDURE

1 Paint the bottom of 2 egg carton cups a color of the rainbow (two cups per color).

2 Cut flat pieces from the other egg carton and draw simple fruit and veggies (e.g., tomatoes, carrots, corn, broccoli, blueberries, eggplant). Color with markers.

3 Glue the fruits and veggies to the corresponding color of your popsicle sticks. Cut the popsicle sticks so they aren't too tall when they stick out of the egg carton.

4 Use scissors to cut a slit on top of each colored egg carton cavity.

HOW TO PLAY

Insert the matching colored stick to each egg cavity. Talk about the various fruits and veggies, how they grow, or what makes a fruit different from a vegetable. What are the different colors of produce?

Learning Skills ▶ Fine motor skills, color recognition, fruit/veggie and planting learning

Tips to Extend Play ▶ Think of a theme other than fruits and veggies. For example, different vehicles or various colored animals would be fun themes.

EGG CARTON GEOBOARD

▲▲▲▲▲▲▲▲▲▲▲▲▲▲▲▲▲▲▲▲▲▲▲▲▲▲▲▲▲▲▲▲▲▲▲▲

Geoboards are great for spatial and early geometric learning. For little ones, geoboards are also fantastic for fine motor skill practice by working and pulling on rubber bands. Make simple shapes with this easy egg carton geoboard. A bonus is that it uses two recyclable materials you likely have at home: egg cartons and pouch lids. The simplicity of this egg carton geoboard makes it a brilliant, creative activity to try at home.

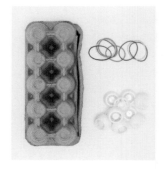

MATERIALS

Egg carton

Craft glue or hot glue gun and hot glue sticks

Food pouch lids

Rubber bands

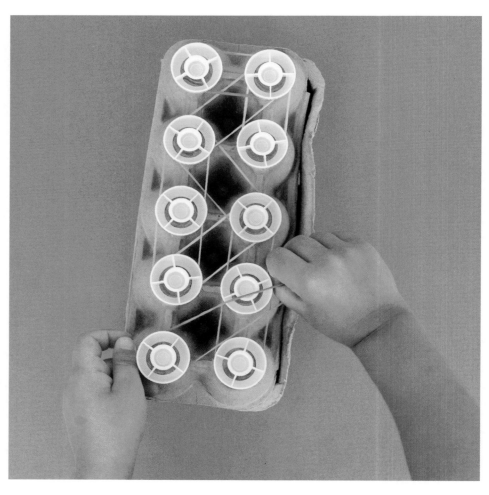

PROCEDURE

1 Glue your pouch lids onto your egg carton. Think about spacing the lids equally, and don't place them too close together.

HOW TO PLAY

Attach rubber bands to the pouch lids to make a fun geoboard. Make shapes, letters, or silly designs.

Learning Skills ▸ Fine motor skills, sensory exploration, cognitive skills

Tips to Extend Play ▸ Instead of rubber bands, thread string around the pouch lids, which may be easier than pulling rubber bands for younger kids.

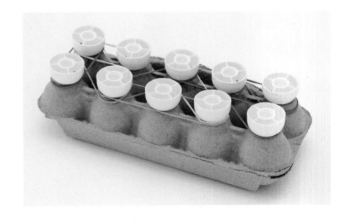

SENSORY DUMP TRUCK

This dump truck craft is full of sensory entertainment. Loading up the back of the truck full of black beans or other small objects is just half the fun. The kids will then get to dump out the contents as a real dump truck does. Once that happens, it's time to pick up the items and load them back into the truck to start all over again.

MATERIALS

Egg carton

Yellow and black paint

Scissors

Pipe cleaner

Craft glue or hot glue gun and hot glue sticks

4 orange lids

Beans or other sensory items

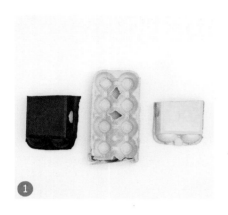

PROCEDURE

1 Separate the top and bottom of the egg carton and paint the bottom cavity (with the cups) yellow. Cut the top part in half and paint one half yellow and the other half black.

2 Thread a pipe cleaner to secure the black half on the bottom yellow egg carton. This ensures you can move the dump truck hauler back and forth.

3 Glue the other half yellow portion on top and glue the lids on as wheels.

HOW TO PLAY

Scoop dried beans on the truck and dump the beans.

Learning Skills ▸ Sensory explorations, fine motor skills

Tips to Extend Play ▸ What else can you scoop and dump to explore with your senses? Fill your dump truck with various sensory items, such as rice and pasta, or nature items, such as twigs, leaves, rocks, or small pinecones.

EGG CARTON FLOWER THREADING

Save those empty egg cartons and make a blooming fine motor craft! The kids can help paint the egg carton flowers in bright and fun colors. Then they get to use their hand-eye coordination to thread in the "stem." This is a great way to create lasting beautiful flowers that require zero maintenance.

MATERIALS

Egg cartons

Scissors

Various colored paints

Paint brushes

Pipe cleaners

PROCEDURE

1 Cut out the bottoms of egg carton cups and create petals by making fringes.

2 Paint the cups to resemble flowers.

3 Poke scissors through the centers.

HOW TO PLAY

Thread the egg carton flowers through the pipe cleaners.

Learning Skills ▶ Fine motor skills, color recognition

Tips to Extend Play ▶ Write letters or numbers on the flower and call them out as you thread. Learn to tie pipe cleaners to create decorative wreaths or garlands.

CHAPTER 8

MARVELOUS MILK CARTONS AND JUGS

▲▲▲▲▲▲

Milk cartons and jugs are so fun because of their playful shapes. Turn cartons into school buses (page 98) and help with the recognition of familiar family faces. The shape of a carton also looks like a roof, so you have a natural canvas for making milk carton houses to learn shapes (page 100). You can also use the natural large cavity of a jug to create a fun sloth toss game (page 102).

HELPFUL HINT Plastic jugs and cartons should be cleaned thoroughly with dish soap and water and left open to dry so moisture is not trapped inside.

MILK CARTON SCHOOL BUS

▲▲▲

Do you have kids who go crazy when they see a yellow school bus? Let them make their own! Using an old milk carton, have the kids create their own bus and then add in pictures of familiar faces. This is a great way to make a fun craft that also doubles as a cute family photo frame. Your kids will be happy to display this on in their room as décor.

MATERIALS

Milk carton

Yellow and black cardstock

Scissors

4 black lids

Craft glue or hot glue gun and hot glue sticks

Printed family photos

PROCEDURE

1 Wrap the milk carton in yellow paper and create windows out of black paper that fit your printed photos. Cut out a window flap from black paper.

2 Glue on the black lids as wheels. Glue on the window flaps and family photos.

HOW TO PLAY

Open the flaps and call out the special family members.

Learning Skills ▸ Social development, cognitive skills

Tips to Extend Play ▸ Instead of family pictures, add photos that teach kids common learning themes, such as animals, shapes, or colors. Or glue on sensory objects to make a sensory-themed bus.

SHAPE MILK CARTON HOUSES

Show your kids that it's easy to upcycle items in your home and turn them into fun crafts full of learning opportunities. Using recycled milk cartons, create fun houses and have children identify the shapes that are used for the doors and windows. Not only will they love creating these tiny houses, they'll also enjoy pointing out all the shapes and colors.

MATERIALS

Milk cartons of various sizes

Craft glue or hot glue gun and hot glue sticks

Colored cardstock

Scissors

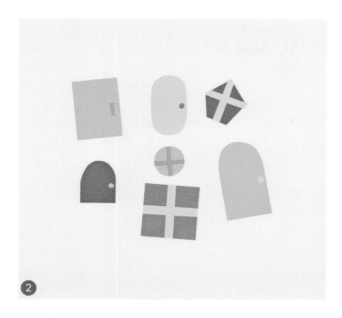

PROCEDURE

1 Use glue to cover your milk cartons with paper.

2 Cut out various windows and doors in different shapes and sizes and glue them to the cartons.

HOW TO PLAY

Identify the colors and shapes of the houses' windows and doors.

Learning Skills Shape and color recognition

Tips to Extend Play Add a personalized element by making windows or doors open and adding a photo of a family member inside for kids to call out and recognize.

SLOTH MILK JUG TOSS

▲▲▲▲▲▲▲▲▲▲▲▲▲▲▲▲▲▲▲▲▲▲▲▲▲▲▲▲▲▲▲▲▲▲▲▲

Preschoolers love cute, sleepy sloths. This tossing activity is a creative way to upcycle jugs while also creating a fun family game. The milk jug makes the perfect sloth body that the kids can help create. Once it's made, you can simply create felt "bean bags" with rice inside to toss into your newly crafted sloth. This is an interactive game that works on many developmental skills at once.

MATERIALS

1 gallon (3.8 L) milk jug, emptied, cleaned, and dried

Craft knife

Cardstock in light brown, dark brown, black, tan, and pink

Scissors

Craft glue or hot glue gun and hot glue sticks

Pencil

Felt scraps in various colors

Rice

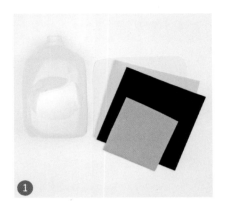

PROCEDURE

1 Cut an opening on the bottom of your jug.

2 Cut your cardstock into a sloth face, adding eyes, cheek, nose, and a tail as shown. Glue the pieces to the jug.

3 Draw small shapes on your felt that will fit inside the jug. Make 2 of each shape and add a small amount of rice in between the 2 shapes. Glue the sides, and those will become your "bean bags."

HOW TO PLAY

Try to throw the bean bags inside the sloth.

Learning Skills Gross motor skills, shapes and color recognition, sensory exploration, cognitive skills

Tips to Extend Play Add sticker numbers to the bean bags. As you throw them inside the sloth, add them up. As you take them out, subtract them.

MILK CARTON BUNNY PLANTERS

▲▲▲▲▲▲▲▲▲▲▲▲▲▲▲▲▲▲▲▲▲▲▲▲▲▲▲▲▲▲▲▲▲▲▲▲▲▲▲

Some "bunny" in the house is certain to love this planter craft. Making these cute milk carton planters is a great way to work on kids' scissor skills while they create delightful and functional planters. This craft is perfect as a spring activity or for anyone who loves bunny rabbits. Plant and watch the greens grow.

MATERIALS

Small milk cartons

White paint or spray paint

Scissors

Pink cardstock

Craft glue or hot glue gun
and hot glue sticks

Black marker

Soil

Small plants

PROCEDURE

1 Paint your milk cartons white. Cut a couple small holes on the bottom for drainage.

2 Cut the cartons into bunny shapes and cut noses and ears out of pink paper.

3 Glue ears and nose on and draw faces with a black marker.

4 Add soil and plants inside the planters.

HOW TO PLAY

Learn about gardening. Cut plants with scissors to develop fine motor skills.

Learning Skills ▸ Gardening, scissor, cutting, and fine motor skills

Tips to Extend Play ▸ What else can you put inside the planters? Can you turn the milk carton into a bunny shape (without cutting the top) and add a hole for a bunny mouth to feed it cardboard carrots?

SIGHT WORDS PEACOCK JUG

▲▲▲▲▲▲▲▲▲▲▲▲▲▲▲▲▲▲▲▲▲▲▲▲▲▲▲▲▲▲▲▲▲▲▲▲▲

It's time to feed the peacock, and he's looking for letters to create sight words on his tail. Recycle a milk jug and create this fun learning activity. All you need to do is create the feathers and add on letters with removable tape. The kids can start to create sight words. Younger kids can simply stuff letters into the milk jug.

MATERIALS

Colored cardstock (yellow, green, blue, black, and white)

Scissors

Milk jug

Craft glue or hot glue gun and hot glue sticks

Black marker

Removable tape

PROCEDURE

1 Cut the papers into peacock parts as shown.

2 Glue the peacock parts onto the milk jug.

3 Cut additional green circles and write letters on them to spell out simple sight words. Place removable tape underneath the paper.

HOW TO PLAY

Say sight words out loud and write them out on the peacock feathers. Or do a simple letter activity by saying a letter out loud and adding that letter on a peacock feather.

Learning Skills ▸ Letter recognition, sight words, fine motor skills

Tips to Extend Play ▸ You can feed the peacock letters, too; it might be easier for younger kids to stuff the circles inside the jug instead of sticking them on the feathers.

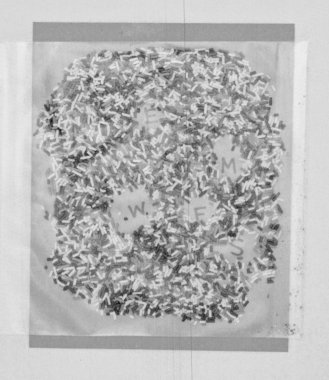

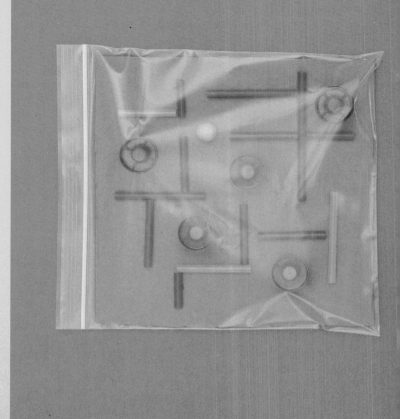

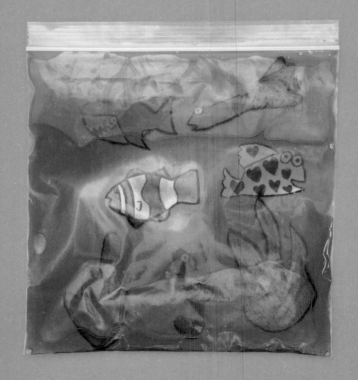

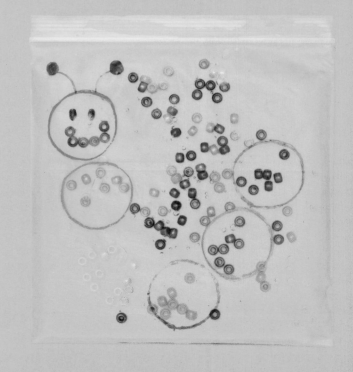

CHAPTER 9

SENSATIONAL SENSORY BAGS

▲▲▲▲▲▲

We love the accessibility and ease of zipper storage bags. It's hard to find a home without them in a kitchen drawer. Since bags are made of plastic and don't biodegrade, it's much more fun to think of another way to reuse them instead of having them sit in a landfill. Fill your caterpillar with matching colored beads (page 110). Make an awesome aquarium dig and hunt for ocean life (page 114) or letters (page 116). The possibilities are endless with this resourceful and inexpensive material.

. . . .

HELPFUL HINTS Removing the labels off zipper bags is easy with rubbing alcohol and a cotton ball or wipe.

If you don't have hair gel to create a sensory activity inside the bag, in most cases, water will work.

Taping the bag down with removable painter's tape can create a more stable way to play.

Use thicker freezer bags for sensory activities since little hands can be rough during play.

Do not reuse zipper bags that have held raw items such as meats. To properly wash your bags, turn them inside out and place them in the top rack of your dishwasher. Or you can submerge in warm, soapy water. Let your bags air dry completely.

. . . .

CATERPILLAR COLOR MATCH

Caterpillars are so much fun. With all their different segments and sections, they're adorable to watch wiggle and are often vividly colored in the imagination of our children. For these reasons, this color bead sensory bag is sure to be a big win among kids. Fill the caterpillar circles with matching colored beads to practice dexterity and color learning.

MATERIALS

Colored markers in rainbow colors (red, orange, yellow, green, blue, purple) and black

Gallon (3.8 L) zipper bag

Hair gel (or water as a substitute; just note it will not be as squishy)

Colored beads in rainbow colors (red, orange, yellow, green, blue, purple)

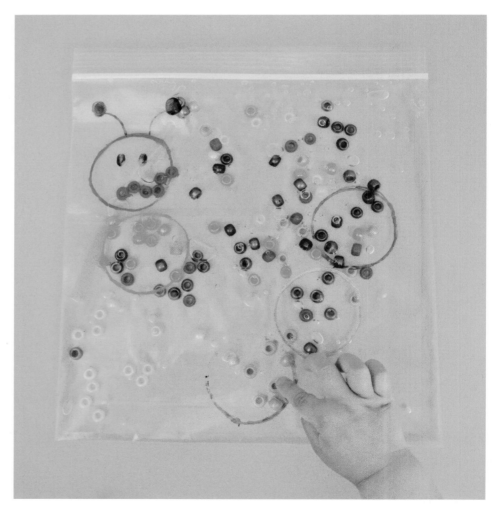

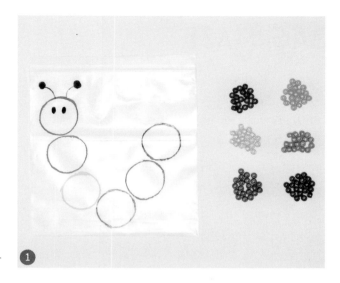

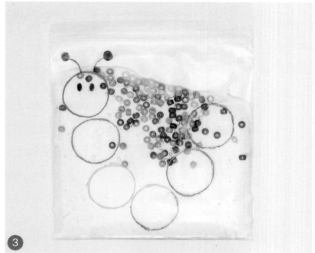

PROCEDURE

1 Draw circular caterpillar segments on top of your zipper bag, starting with a red head and moving on to orange, yellow, green, blue, and purple segments. Add black eyes and antennas.

2 Fill about half the bag with hair gel. Smooth it out evenly.

3 Add your colored beads inside.

HOW TO PLAY

Ask your child to use their fingers to add the right colored beads inside each caterpillar circle. For example, push the red beads inside the red circle.

Learning Skills ▸ Color recognition, fine motor skills

Tips to Extend Play ▸ You can draw colored shapes instead of a caterpillar and add some shape learning. You can also try using different objects other than small beads to make moving the items more challenging or easier, depending on the age of your child.

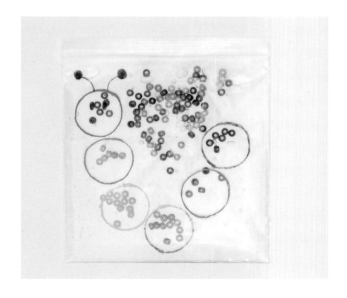

SENSORY BAG MAZE

▲▲▲

Mazes are always a ton of fun, but when combined with sensory activities, they're a creative and new interactive idea. This Sensory Bag Maze will have the kids solving the puzzle with both their hands and minds. We kept this one open-ended to make it easy for little ones, so there is no beginning or end, but you can make it more difficult with a start and finish. Kids can focus on following the maze with their eyes to get to the end and then use their hands to guide the pompom on the correct path. This activity is great for visual learning and analytical thinking.

MATERIALS

Straws

Scissors

Pouch lids

Flat piece of cardboard that fits inside the bag

Craft glue or hot glue gun and hot glue sticks

Gallon (3.8 L) zipper bag

Small pompom or marble

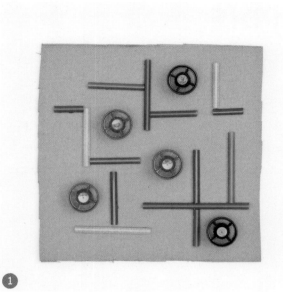

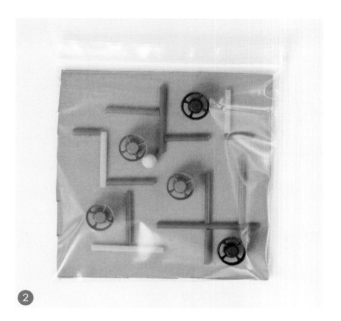

PROCEDURE

1 Cut straws into various lengths and lay them out along with the lids to make a maze on top of your cardboard. Glue the pieces down.

2 Insert the cardboard inside your bag and add a pompom or marble. Zip the bag shut.

HOW TO PLAY

Push the pompom along the straws and around the pouch lids. Name the straw and pouch lid colors as you go along.

Learning Skills ▶ Fine motor skills, color recognition, cognitive skills, sensory exploration

Tips to Extend Play ▶ Add dot stickers on the cardboard with numbers or letters and ask them to push the marble or pompom to the letter or number you call out.

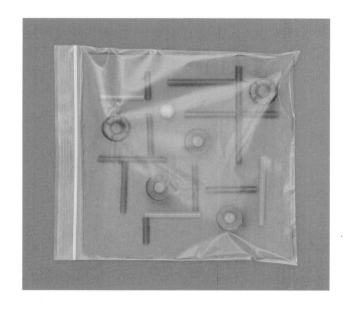

AQUARIUM DIG

This sensory bag aquarium dig is great for exploring and using imagination. Use this sensory activity as a perfect way for early learners to have a fun digging experience (and without the mess, too). Using a plastic bag filled with hair gel and food coloring, kids can look through the "ocean" to dig for the cardboard fish hiding underneath. This activity is great for fine motor skills as well as exploratory play.

MATERIALS

Scrap cardboard

Scissors

Markers or paint

Hair gel (or water as a substitute; just note it will not be as squishy)

Gallon (3.8 L) zipper bag

Blue food coloring

12" x 12" (30.5 x 30.5 cm) blue cardstock paper

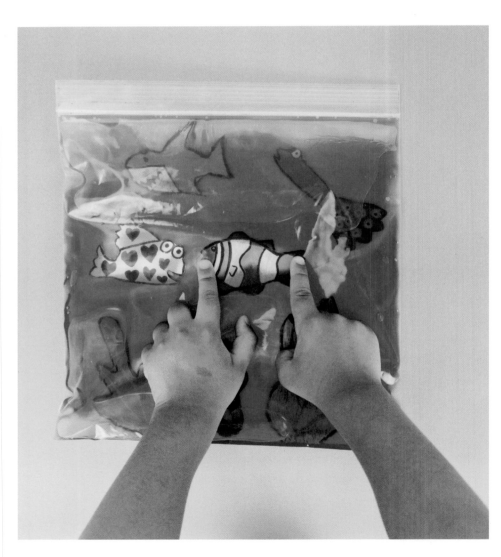

PROCEDURE

1 Cut fish and sea life shapes from your scrap cardboard and color them to make vibrant sea creatures.

2 Place half a bag's worth of hair gel inside your bag and add enough food coloring to get a blue color. Zip the bag shut. Mix the gel around until the blue food coloring is evenly distributed.

3 Place your cardboard sea creatures on top of your blue cardstock and then place your bag on top of the ocean scene.

HOW TO PLAY

Have your child use their fingers to dig, explore, and find fish by spreading out the blue "water" and finding the sea life. Call out the creatures' names and talk about different sea critters.

Learning Skills ▶ Fine motor skills, animal/sea life learning, sensory exploration

Tips to Extend Play ▶ You can write numbers or letters on the fish and have them search for the ones you call out. You can color the fish one color and have them dig for that to create a fun color recognition game.

SPRINKLES SENSORY LETTER HUNT

Sprinkles can be used for more than just treats. Write down letters of the alphabet on paper and put them under a bag filled with sprinkles. Make certain the bag is sealed and then let the kids go on a letter hunt by using their fingers to open up the sprinkles. This is an exciting way to practice dexterity and learn letters.

MATERIALS

Black marker

Colored paper

Sprinkles

Gallon (3.8 L) zipper bag

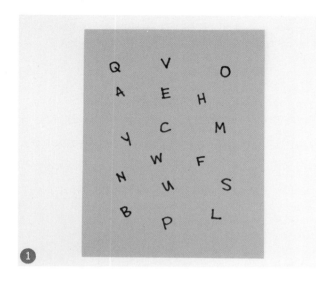

PROCEDURE

1 Write letters on the colored paper.

2 Place sprinkles inside the bag.

3 Place the paper underneath the bag.

HOW TO PLAY

Hunt for letters and call them out by "digging" through the sprinkles with your fingers.

Learning Skills ▸ Letter recognition, fine motor skills

Tips to Extend Play ▸ Instead of letters, try numbers or other learning elements, such as simple shapes, or draw common objects, such as cup, ball, or spoon.

DINOSAUR SENSORY BAG

Calling all dinosaur fans! This fun cardboard cutout activity is perfect for sensory play. Fill the bag with a bit of hair gel, add in colorful pompoms, and let the kids use their fine motor skills to push the pompoms to fill out the dinosaur body, all while keeping this a mess-free activity. This interactive sensory activity for kids is also great for learning colors by adding various colored pompoms.

MATERIALS

Cardboard

Craft knife

Markers or crayons

Gallon (3.8 L) zipper bag

Hair gel (or water as a substitute; just note it will not be as squishy)

Pompoms

PROCEDURE

1 Cut out a dinosaur shape from your cardboard. On the original piece of cardboard, draw and color the dinosaur's spikes and feet.

2 Fill about half the bag with hair gel and add pompoms.

3 Lay the cardboard over the bag and add a smile on the bag with a black marker.

HOW TO PLAY

Push the pompoms inside the dinosaur to complete its body.

Learning Skills ▸ Fine motor skills, sensory exploration, color recognition

Tips to Extend Play ▸ Add some fun number learning by asking your child to add a certain number of pompoms inside the dinosaur's body.

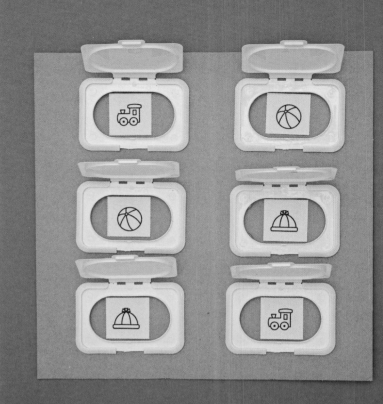

WHAT

ARE   WITH   YOU

THIS   CAN

AND

CHAPTER 10

WONDERFUL WIPE LID ACTIVITIES

▲▲▲▲▲▲

If you have preschool-aged children, chances are you're still carrying around baby wipes beyond the baby phase. Most parents would agree baby wipes are great for so many uses other than for diapers. They are quick fixes for wiping dirty mouths, hands, or messes on the table or floor. With so many wipe lids around, you'll find yourself wondering what to do with them. Here are some fun ideas. Why not make a sensory board (page 122) and engage your littles ones in exploring different textures? Or create a fun memory matching game (page 126) or monster box for learning sight words (page 130)?

....

HELPFUL HINTS Remove the wipe lids cleanly from the container when you're done with the wipes and bundle the lids together with a rubber band. When you need a wipe lid, it will be easy to find.

....

SENSORY BOARD

▲▲▲

Children love to explore different sensory textures at this age. They also love to play peekaboo. This wipe lid board takes advantage of both delights by providing a sensory peekaboo experience. Kids will love flipping lids to reveal a unique and creative texture. They will love running their fingers through the different feel of wool, felt, and feathers and will also point out the various colors.

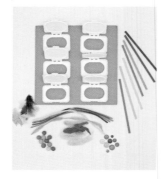

MATERIALS

6 baby wipe lids

1 12" (30.5 cm) cardboard square

Craft glue or hot glue gun and hot glue sticks

Various rainbow-colored sensory items (We used pipe cleaners, pompoms, buttons, felt flowers, feathers, and wool)

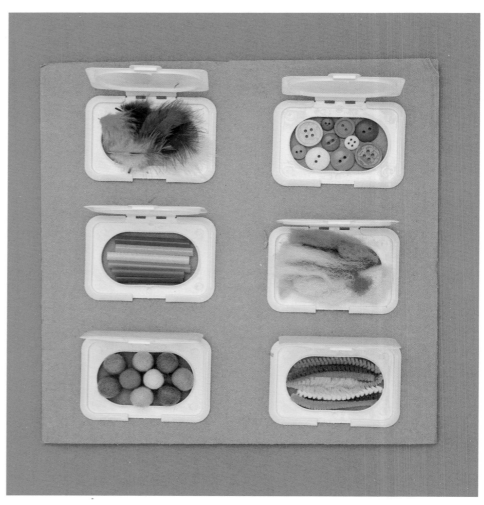

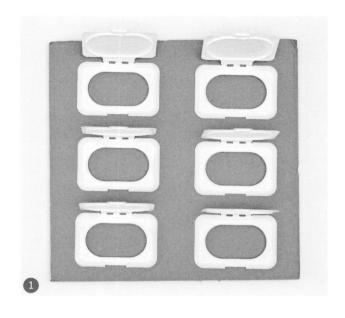 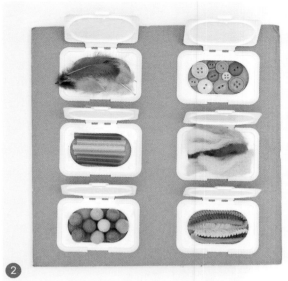

PROCEDURE

1 Glue your wipe lids on the cardboard base, 2 across.

2 Open the lids and add the materials inside the lids. Once you have the items in place, glue each securely.

HOW TO PLAY

Open the lids and touch the materials. Ask your child what the texture feels like. Soft, rough, or smooth? How would they describe the touch? Point out the colors of the materials.

Learning Skills ▸ Fine motor skills, color recognition, sensory exploration

Tips to Extend Play ▸ Instead of gluing down items, you can tape contact sticker paper and lay down the items instead. This way, you can have your child practice more fine motor skills by taking the items out and extend learning by swapping out new sensory items to explore.

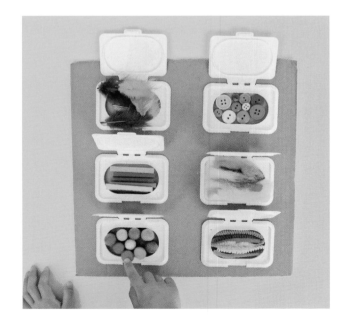

WIPE LID PHOTO HOUSES

A house is a comforting place for little kids that makes them feel safe. Family pictures are a great way to extend that comfort and help your child recognize members of the family. Using wipe lids and popsicle sticks to create tiny houses, you can then add family photos inside. When your child lifts the lid, they'll see familiar faces that are certain to make them smile.

MATERIALS

Popsicle sticks

Wipe lids

Craft glue or hot glue gun and hot glue sticks

Flat piece of cardboard

Photos

PROCEDURE

1 Create houses with your popsicle sticks; use the lids as doors. Glue onto your cardboard.

2 Cut out photos to fit in your door and glue them on.

HOW TO PLAY

Have kids open the houses and name their friends and family members.

Learning Skills ▸ Fine motor skills, social and cognitive skills, memory

Tips to Extend Play ▸ Instead of photos, replace them with learning elements such as shapes, colors, numbers, or letters. Have kids call out what they see.

MATCHING MEMORY GAME

Kids get so excited when they find a matching pair. Setting up this wipe lid memory game is super easy because you only need lids and cardboard. We used clip art with kid-friendly items, but you can easily draw your own. Or use letters, numbers, shapes, or simple words. The possibilities are endless with this fun matching activity.

MATERIALS

Cardboard

Wipe lids

Craft glue or hot glue gun and hot glue sticks

Scissors

Printout of kid-friendly clip art or drawn items

Removable tape

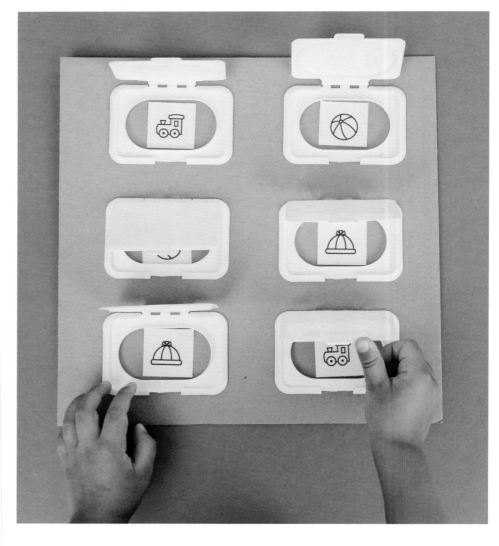

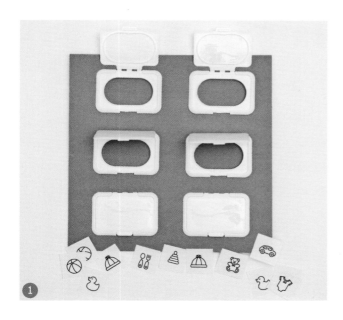

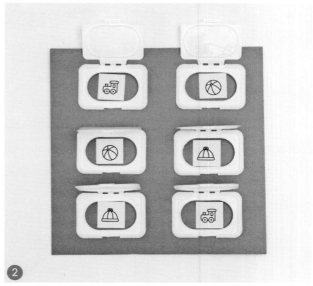

PROCEDURE

1 Glue your wipe lids to the cardboard and make sure there is an even number as you will need 2 lids per pair of drawings.

2 Cut your clip art or drawing and use removable tape to add them to the wipe lids. Using removable tape means you can create multiple versions of this simple matching game.

HOW TO PLAY

Have your child flip open the lids and find the matching picture.

Learning Skills ▸ Cognitive skills, fine motor skills, memory, object recognition

Tips to Extend Play ▸ Instead of clip art, use words, letters, shapes, or colored sticker dots to learn colors. Or match lower- and uppercase letters.

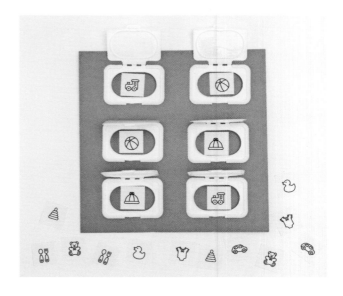

WIPE LID YARN PULL

▲▲

This wipe lid yarn pull activity is a fine motor activity that will keep your child entertained. Children will enjoy pulling out the brightly colored yarns and sorting them according to color. They will also enjoy the texture and sensory feel of various yarns and wools. All you really need for this fantastic sensory project is a recycled wipe lid, a box, and yarn.

MATERIALS

Food box

Craft knife

Wipe lid

Craft glue or hot glue gun and hot glue sticks

Yarn

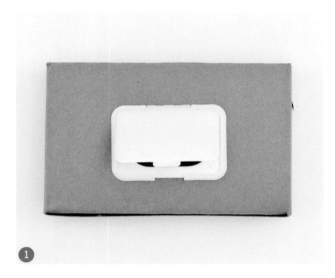

PROCEDURE

1 Cut an opening on the front of the box and glue your wipe lid over it.

2 Place yarn inside the box.

HOW TO PLAY

Pull yarn out of the box. Call out the color of the yarn.

Learning Skills ▸ Fine motor skills, color recognition

Tips to Extend Play ▸ Instead of yarn, make the box a "mystery sensory box" and add fun objects kids can guess by sensing and feeling before pulling out

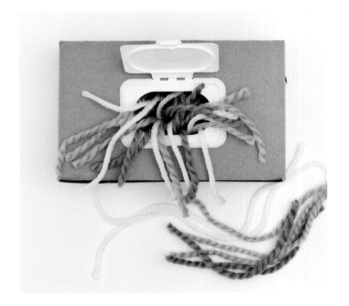

MONSTER LID SIGHT WORDS

▲▲▲▲▲▲▲▲▲▲▲▲▲▲▲▲▲▲▲▲▲▲▲▲▲▲▲▲▲▲▲▲▲▲▲▲

This sight word monster is hungry, and he needs food fast. The kids will get a kick out of feeding the hungry monster while they learn their sight words at the same time. All you need to create this monster activity is an empty box, paper, and a lid from a container of wipes. The kids can easily help with decorating the monster with bright colors.

MATERIALS

Empty food box

Green, blue, white, and black cardstock

Craft glue or hot glue gun and hot glue sticks

Scissors

Black marker

Wipe lid

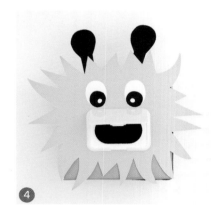

PROCEDURE

1 Wrap the food box in blue paper and glue the paper onto the box.

2 Cut the remaining paper into a monster face as shown and write sight words with a black marker on pieces of white paper.

3 Cut a hole the size of your wipe lid on the box and glue the lid over it.

4 Glue the monster parts over the box.

HOW TO PLAY

Feed the monster sight words by saying them and inserting them in his mouth.

Learning Skills ▸ Sight words, fine motor skills

Tips to Extend Play ▸ Instead of sight words, write letters, numbers, or shapes. Use various colored papers to learn colors. Add loose parts and have kids shake the box and guess what is inside for sensory exploration.

ACKNOWLEDGMENTS

▲▲▲▲▲▲▲▲▲▲▲▲▲▲▲▲▲▲▲▲▲▲▲▲▲▲▲▲▲▲▲▲▲▲▲▲

Writing a book is a labor of love that starts long before the first words on a page are written. In my case it starts with my husband, Tim, who gave me the unconditional support and love eight years ago to start my creative kids' website, Hello, Wonderful (www.hellowonderful.co). It was powered over the years by endless creative projects with my children, Alia, Kian, and Dashiell, who are my heart and muse. Our creativity has been shared passionately with families across the world. This community of creative families and their support on my blog and social media continue to encourage me to create playful activities. The joy in inspiring families to bond meaningfully when creating with their children is the reason why I love what I do.

The specific subject nature of this book, *Recycle and Play*, would not have existed without the amazing Instagram community @recycleandplay, co-founded with my dear friend and creative co-collaborator, Myriam @mothercould. Myriam has supported the writing of this book from day one and is a champion of easy, no-mess recycled activities in her own widely popular community.

Creating a meaningful business through blogging can be lonely, which is why I'm eternally grateful for my blogging buddies "I'm Crafty and You Know It" group, Kim, Melissa, Maggy, Kate, Susie, Penny, Chelsey, Rodrigo, Sam, Kate, Stef, Emma, Helen, Rachel, Bonnie, and Andreja. Over the years, we have supported each other through endless blogging challenges and successes. Many have authored their own books. Their advice and support were invaluable to me as a first-time author.

The actual process of writing a book full of creative projects takes time. My dear friend Kat is my crafting partner-in-crime and carried my hands through the entire creative journey while literally helping me cut paper tubes, cardboard, and milk jugs. Everyone should have a mom friend like Kat who supports them 100%!

The beautiful photography you see here is credited to my talented photographer friend Ning (www.ningwong.com). His heart and all-encompassing kindness transcends the beauty he creates in each photograph.

Thank you to the adorable children you see photographed in this book. Nikky, Lena, Reygan, Emily, Rafi, and Dashiell, you were all so patient and cute.

To the incredible team at Quarto Book Publishing, Jonathan, my acquiring editor; Marissa, art director; and Mel, marketing manager: Thank you for believing in my vision and bringing it to life.

ABOUT THE AUTHOR

Agnes Hsu is a playful mom of three who resides in sunny Southern California. She is the founder of the popular creative website for kids Hello, Wonderful, which has inspired families over the last eight years with simple colorful kids' crafts and activities. She is also the co-founder of the highly engaged Instagram community @RecycleandPlay.

Agnes believes everyone has a creative soul and that creativity doesn't require amazing talents or fancy materials. Learning and play should be fun and simple for kids and parents. The meaningful stuff comes in making memories and raising kids to become curious and imaginative explorers on their own.

Get inspired to create with your kids by visiting Agnes's creative and playful website, www.hellowonderful.co, or follow her Instagrams @hellowonderful_co and @recycleandplay.

INDEX